AN

Alchemy

OF

Genres

Cross-Genre

Writing

by American

Feminist

Poet-Critics

Feminist Issues: Practice, Politics, Theory

Kathleen M. Balutansky and Alison Booth, editors

Carol Siegel, *Lawrence among the Women: Wavering Boundaries in Women's Literary Traditions*

Harriet Blodgett, *Capacious Hold-All: An Anthology of Englishwomen's Diary Writings*

Joy Wiltenburg, *Disorderly Women and Female Power in the Popular Literature of Early Modern England and Germany*

Diane P. Freedman, *An Alchemy of Genres: Cross-Genre Writing by American Feminist Poet-Critics*

AN

Alchemy

OF

Genres

Cross-Genre

Writing

by American

Feminist

Poet-Critics

DIANE P. FREEDMAN

University Press of Virginia
Charlottesville and London

THE UNIVERSITY PRESS OF VIRGINIA
Copyright © 1992 by the Rector and Visitors
of the University of Virginia

First published 1992

Library of Congress Cataloguing-in-Publication Data

Freedman, Diane P.
    An alchemy of genres : cross-genre writing by American feminist
poet-critics / Diane P. Freedman.
        p.   cm. — (Feminist issues)
    Includes bibliographical references.
    ISBN 0-8139-1377-2. — ISBN 0-8139-1378-0 (pbk.)
    1. Feminism and literature—United States—History—20th
century.   2. Women and literature—United States—History—
20th century.   3. American poetry—Women authors—History and
criticism.   4. Criticism—United States—History—20th century.
5. Feminist literary criticism—United States.   6. Literary
form.   I. Title.   II. Series: Feminist issues (Charlottesville, Va.)
PS152.F74   1992
811.009'9287—dc20   91-39000
                                                              CIP

Printed in the United States of America

The golden light of metaphor, which is the intelligence of poetry, was implicit in alchemical study. To change, magically, one substance into another, more valuable one is the ancient function of metaphor, as it was of alchemy.

Patricia Hampl, *A Romantic Education*

We need to support each other in rejecting the limitations of a tradition—a manner of reading, of speaking, of writing, of criticizing—which was never really designed to include us at all.

Adrienne Rich, "Toward a More Feminist Criticism"

Feminist criticism itself, in an effort to "push against" the logic of discourse, drifts toward the narrative. . . . In this case, criticism takes literature as its object, yes: but here literature in a different sense is likely to become the subject, the feminist critic, the woman writer, the woman herself.

Mary Jacobus, "Men of Maxims and *The Mill on the Floss*"

In the process of working on women writers, I had changed my critical persona, style, function, and stance from "masculine" to "feminine." I had exchanged the authoritative for the tentative, the impositional for the instrumental, and the antagonist for the lover. . . . If I did what I set out to do right, my words would rapidly become obsolete, overwritten by the dialogue they had started.

Judith Fetterley, Introduction to *Provisions*

Raised as we have been on generations of critical one-upmanship, with many of our mentors delighting in subtle putdown or in contentious nastiness, we need not ourselves follow in that style; indeed it is a style which stands as anathema to the very idealism of the women's movement as a whole. Let us therefore openly admit that our enterprise is a new one, . . . and that, consequently, those of us engaged in the enterprise, with all its experimentation, will occa-

sionally commit errors of judgment, make mistakes, and hopefully, grow and change along with the enterprise we are in the process of creating.

> Annette Kolodyny, "Some Notes on Defining a 'Feminist Literary Criticism'"

Q: Might feminism be a force for reviving the poet-critic?
A: I hope so.

> "Feminist Criticism in the University: An Interview with Sandra Gilbert"

Contents

Acknowledgments

I wish to express particular appreciation to Carolyn Allen, who formally introduced me to feminist criticism and theory, thereafter tolerating my informality in prose style; to my students, without whose endless expository essays I might not have come to re-form and reaffirm the creative-critical amalgam; and to the writers whose words and examples are invoked throughout the book. For encouragement and suggestions, I am further indebted to Vicki Ekanger, Barbara Ryan, and Jerry Cobb; Mark Patterson, Evan Watkins, and Donna Gerstenberger; Martha Stoddard Holmes, Steve Osborne, Karen Shabetai, Olivia Frey, Gloria Anzaldúa, and Nancy Essig, my editor at the University Press of Virginia. Special thanks go to Catherine Gjerdingen for her careful readings and assistance. Most of all, for being there for the long haul, I thank my husband, Brian McWilliams, and the members of our two families, especially my parents, Mary Spock Freedman and Albert Leon Freedman, and my grandmother, Ruth Silverstein Freedman. This book is dedicated to them.

"The Performance" first appeared in *Permafrost* (1985).

"The Way the Gravestones Align" first appeared in *Matrix* (1985).

"The Butterfly" first appeared in *Transition* (1979).

The author gratefully acknowledges permission to reprint passages from the following works:

Excerpts from "A Talk: Convocation 1972" and "In Search of Our Mothers' Gardens" in *In Search of Our Mothers' Gardens:*

1983 by Cherrie Moraga. Excerpted with permission from the author and from the publisher, South End Press, 116 Saint Botolph Street, Boston, MA 02115.

"Motheroot" from *Abiding Appalachia: Where Mountain and Atom Meet* by Marilou Awiakta. Used by permission of St. Lukes Press.

"Out of the Rubbish" from *My Mother's Body* by Marge Piercy. Copyright © 1985 by Marge Piercy. Reprinted by permission of Alfred A. Knopf, Inc., and the Wallace Literary Agency, Inc.

"Power" is reprinted from *The Fact of a Doorframe: Poems Selected and New, 1950–1984,* by Adrienne Rich, by permission of the author and W. W. Norton & Company, Inc. Copyright © 1984 by Adrienne Rich. Copyright © 1975, 1978 by W. W. Norton & Company, Inc. Copyright © 1981 by Adrienne Rich.

"The Rose and the Eagle" from *The Twelve-Spoked Wheel Flashing* by Marge Piercy. Copyright © 1977, 1978 by Middlemarsh, Inc. Reprinted by permission of the Wallace Literary Agency, Inc.

"Seedlings in the Mail" from *Circles on the Water* by Marge Piercy. Copyright © 1982 by Marge Piercy. Reprinted by permission of Alfred A. Knopf, Inc., and the Wallace Literary Agency, Inc.

"Sudden Journey" from *Willingly* by Tess Gallagher. Copyright © 1984 Tess Gallagher. Reprinted with the permission of Graywolf Press.

Abbreviations

BBP   Adrienne Rich, *Blood, Bread, and Poetry: Selected Prose 1979–1985*

COW   Marge Piercy, *Circles on the Water*

FD   Adrienne Rich, *The Fact of a Doorframe: Poems Selected and New 1950–1984*

LSS   Adrienne Rich, *On Lies, Secrets, and Silence: Selected Prose 1966–1978*

MFE   Susan Griffin, *Made from This Earth*

MG   Alice Walker, *In Search of Our Mothers' Gardens*

MMB   Marge Piercy, *My Mother's Body: Poems*

PCB   Marge Piercy, *Parti-Colored Blocks for a Quilt*

TSW   Marge Piercy, *The Twelve-Spoked Wheel Flashing*

AN

Alchemy

OF

Genres

Cross-Genre

Writing

by American

Feminist

Poet-Critics

ONE

Discourse as Power: Renouncing Denial

[Marie Curie] died   a famous woman   denying
her wounds
denying
her wounds   came   from the same source as her power
Adrienne Rich, "Power" (1974)

The majority of women who go through
undergraduate and graduate school suffer an
intellectual coercion of which they are not
even consciously aware. In a world where
language and naming are power, silence is
oppression, is violence.
Adrienne Rich, "Conditions for Work: The
Common World of Women" (1976)

Your silence will not protect you.
Audre Lorde, "The Transformation of
Silence into Language and Action" (1977)

I will no longer be made to feel ashamed of
existing. I will have my voice: Indian,
Spanish, White. I will have my serpent's
tongue—my woman's voice, my sexual voice, my
poet's voice. I will overcome the tradition
of silence.
Gloria Anzaldúa, *Borderlands/La Frontera*
(1987)

Long before I embarked on this project to seek out and characterize feminist strategies in literary writing, I was aware of the connection between words and power. I did not see the possible wounding effect of certain kinds of discourse; I accepted blithely the classical notion of language as power. To survive in Athenian democracy, where (male) citizens argued their own cases and lawsuits were a way of life, men had to become adept orators. If they couldn't speak well enough, they hired coaches or speech writers to augment their education in reading, writing, and oratory. I thought I should be prepared for my days as citizen—study English or attend law school, or both. I hadn't yet recognized that as a woman I was alienated by both tradition and temperament from conventional argumentative discourse; I only vaguely sensed why it was an emotional struggle for me to read and write in what I later found out has been called the "male" or "logocentric" or even "phallogocentric" mode. I believed I could use what I took to be my increasing facility with language to give voice to whatever bothered or drew me. I never thought it might be the language and laws of patriarchy that did the "wounding" and excluding.

Like Marie Curie in Adrienne Rich's poem excerpted above, I couldn't see or I denied that my wounds might come from the same source as my power, that there was a cost for conventional power. In Curie's case, the source was radium, that odd element which both cures and causes cancers. In my case, it was language. Language can liberate but it can also reinscribe, reiterate oppression. Like Curie with her radiation-caused cataracts, I didn't see the circle in which I was caught: use writing to "think like a man" and suffer; ignore the prison of patriarchal language at my peril.

My project as a whole investigates what Thomas J. Farrell, Pamela Annas, Mary DeShazer, and others call the *female* mode—a style associative, nonhierarchical, personal, and open-ended—particularly as it is practiced by (though it is not limited to) feminist poet-critics.[1] Writers in this mode use language not to gain power but to create intimacy (Thorne, Kramarae, Henley 15), intimacy often achieved through self-reflexive statements on the why and how of their practice. Such

metadiscursive comments commonly announce the substitu-
tion of unconventional or multiple genres for the traditional
essay, argue for personal over fixed forms.

"Why we write, as feminists, is not separable from our
lives," claims Susan Griffin (*MFE* 220). "In looking at this book
[*Borderlands/La Frontera*], that I'm almost finished writing, I
see a mosaic pattern (Aztec-like) emerging" (66), writes Gloria
Anzaldúa, ever conscious of her multiple identities and heritage
(Mexican/Indian/Anglo/black/lesbian/feminist/poet/essayist/
autobiographer). She theorizes that a "mestiza" like her (a per-
son of mixed Indian and Spanish blood) in a constant state of
"mental nepantilism" ("an Aztec word meaning torn between
two ways") "has to shift out of habitual formations; from con-
vergent thinking, analytical reasoning that tends to use ra-
tionality to move toward a single goal (a Western mode), to
divergent thinking, characterized by movement away from set
patterns and goals toward a more whole perspective, one that
includes rather than excludes" (78–79).

These writings elaborate what has indeed become a tenet of
feminist criticism: the personal is the political. But I am contin-
ually struck by the gap between the writing read and the writ-
ing written in graduate classes and academic journals. Jane
Tompkins, a critic feeling increasingly shackled by academic-
critical conventions, reports: "It is a tenet of feminist rhetoric
that the personal is the political, but who in the academy acts on
this where language is concerned? We all speak the father
tongue, which is impersonal, while decrying the father's ideas"
("Me and My Shadow" 174). Refusing to give up or deny myself
feminist forms (as Tompkins also refuses in her article), how-
ever, I have discovered more and more personal, mixed-genre,
metadiscursive writers published by more and more journals or
presses. They challenge the critical canon with their "common"
language and hybrid, alchemical forms as much as they do any
other canon. I praise them for refusing to deny their personal
histories or the process by which they come to know what they
know or to believe what they believe. Combining poet with
critic, they join private and public, writer and reader, and past

and present as they experiment with and announce a blending of traditional genres, (poetry, autobiography, drama, fiction, among them), subgenres (free-verse lyrics, fables, epigrams, diaries, exhortation), and disciplinary discourses. Mixed, crossed, or blurred genres is my shorthand way of referring to such anomalous, self-conscious blendings.

As Farrell puts it, "The female mode seems at times to obfuscate the boundary between the self of the author and the subject of the discourse, as well as between the self and the audience" (910). Moreover, its stylistic preference is for writing that "follows the shifting perspectives of the writer's mind" (Huber, reviewing Annas 356). Again and again, feminist poet-critics speak about refusing to be silenced, not only historically and by patriarchy in general, but within the privileged enclave of academia and its discourses, to which at least some feminists have had token or illusory access. As Adrienne Rich asserts, no woman is an insider in the institutions fathered by masculine consciousness. Contemporary feminists want their voices heard in the academy as well as in society, but they write and speak increasingly on and in their own terms, in language denouncing dominant institutions and their discourse(s) while renouncing self-denial. Such writers refuse to deny their many voices; they speak *of* as well as *from* the self, thus demonstrating the power engendered by feminist discourse(s) while rejecting "male" versions of powerful discourse.[2]

If why and how women write is not separable from their lives, it is also not separable from a history of silence and the nonacademic forms of expression that served lives formerly (and formally) circumscribed. Julia Penelope (Stanley) and Susan J. Wolfe maintain, "The women of the 20th century who write speak out of a tradition of silence, a tradition of the . . . personal, revelatory language of diaries and journals. Our style, therefore, does not conform to the traditional patriarchal style we have been taught to regard as 'literary' and 'correct'" (125). The histories of silenced and censored women, continuing of course even when all American women were allegedly given access to literary education, the vote, the press, and professorships, became fully known to me only after I became a doctoral candidate in English and began to ask: What kinds of discourse yield (or reject) what kinds of power?

Before I decided to pursue a doctorate in English, however, I considered attending law school, gaining power through conventional oratory. An administrative assistant, I worked at a university with a law school, and one weekend, in order to learn what law school and the practice of law would be like, I attended a symposium on women and the law offered by the Women's Law Caucus. Of the many activities in which I took part that weekend, one stands out: I see now that it offers a matrix for explaining and exploring my alternately assertive and ambivalent views of the power of discourse(s).

I joined a small group role-playing situations that lawyers who are committed to women's rights might face. What if a manufacturing company notorious for discriminatory hiring and promotion practices asked a feminist law firm, of which we were members, to conduct a one-day workshop on sexual harassment? We and our partners knew the workshop would bring in a big fee, and we were short on the funds needed to help the clients to whom we were most committed—women and children on welfare, the homeless, rape victims. But we also knew the workshop was merely a PR move for the company. It was unlikely management would follow through or support victims of sexual harassment. The workshop was just for show, and hiring our firm was just a token gesture. Would we do the workshop anyway?

Many women said they would always refuse to work for such a firm; their valuable time would be wasted, especially since no program was planned as a follow-up to the workshop. They refused to be part of the engineered corporate hypocrisy. But I felt strongly that the women in the unenlightened corporation—not to mention the pro-bono cases the workshop fee would make possible—needed our help. Even in the absence of a full-fledged employee assistance program or even a company ombudsperson, women furnished with language describing their oppression would be empowered to stop harassers, I argued. Many women don't even know the term and therefore don't have the concept of *sexual harassment*. They might know they feel uncomfortable when pressured by a male coworker or supervisor for sex but, ignorant of the word for it, might not know how many others are fighting similar situations. Sexual harassment itself is an institutional, not merely individual, phenomenon; the term itself, like a workshop, signals that there are laws against it and measures that can be taken against those who "sexually harass."

The general term may also flatten out the differences between its sufferers, deny the depths and details of the particular, unless the naming process is a prelude to a narrative one, an exchanging and validating of individual stories and voices. In fact, women may learn more through personal narratives— their own and others'—than through an argumentative discourse based on generalities and abstractions alone.[3] But this general term, probably coined by women lawyers, must be better than none, I thought, and I told my story.

I confided that when I was a sophomore in college, a male professor had in fact harassed me, but I didn't know how to speak of it to my friends, male or female. (I had been sitting in a stiff wooden chair in his office, discussing the opportunity for a grant for summer fieldwork, when the professor strode from behind his desk to silence me with a sudden violent kiss, in the middle of which I sputtered awkwardly that I had to go.) I thought it was my fault. I was helped along in my silence by my profound embarrassment and the fact that I needed the grant, but after running that day down the halls of the department the professor chaired, I soon changed my academic major. When harassed again, if more subtly, by two other male professors, I still couldn't generalize from the first experience, lump the incidents together under one rubric, one name. If I had had a term for this phenomenon, however, I feel sure I could have not only stopped these men from future acts of harassment but felt less anxious and confused.

As I was to read later in an interview with poet Marge Piercy, "When you're a woman before there is a language of feminism, trying to understand what it's like to be a woman, you have no concepts, no vocabulary for even understanding your own situation" (*PCB* 324). Those hypothetical women of our workshop—and others like me at nineteen—needed to know the term *harassment,* needed to recognize and acquire the power of naming rather than denial. They needed also to share their stories. As Griffin notes, "Silence leads to more silence." Joining a conversation in many ways begun by Tillie Olsen's classic essay "Silences in Literature" (and continued by such works as Joanna Russ's *How to Suppress Women's Writing*), Griffin explains, "Even though I wrote, I could not write about my own life, a woman's life. Instead, I kept my own kind of silence by writing in what I thought was an acceptable way, about the world in which men live" (*MFE* 186).

My decision to investigate and then apply to law school came from the anger I'd felt at being denied a voice even in the world of the English major (in classes with male teachers, as a public- and private-school teacher, as an underpaid freelance editor and proofreader, and as a poet myself—a role considered by others flaky, out of touch with reality), as well as from the conviction that I could "master" the law and its language. I believed I could help save others both with and from legal language. Like Rich, I was someone for whom language had implied freedom while I nonetheless recognized that others "have had language and literature *used against* them, to keep them in their place, to mystify, to bully, to make them feel powerless" (Teaching Language," *LSS* 63). I supposed back then that learning the terms of the system was the first step toward surviving under it, and that survival was required for change from within or without.

I see now that we would have received a better education in naming at the hands of a woman poet than a lawyer, since the dictionary defines *harassment* as merely "annoyance" or "vexation." Dominant language can help, because it does foreground the transgression better than silence and it makes possible group knowledge, group response. But it is still somehow inadequate for the hustling/hassling scandal of a person in power taking advantage of someone socially, economically, physically, and verbally unempowered. I wish not only that I had known of a term or a university policy for what happened, but that I had had access to Rich's analysis, which came, in 1978, too late for me. Rich's words certainly clearly narrate my experience: "Most young women experience a profound mixture of humiliation and self-doubt over seductive gestures by men who have the power to award grades, open doors to grants and graduate school, or extend special knowledge and training. Even turned aside, such gestures constitute mental rape, destructive to a woman's ego. They are acts of domination, as despicable as the molestation of the daughter by the father" ("Taking Women Students Seriously," *LSS* 248).

I had always been an advocate, someone who helped stage a moratorium against the Vietnam War in my junior high school, tried to suspend classes in high school to hold a symposium called "Future Week," built a "free school" within the physical structure and curriculum of our high school, took buses to Washington, D.C., for impeach-Nixon and antinuclear rallies. I was also a rather irritable consumer advocate, one who wrote angry but businesslike letters to manufacturers whose products failed me (I was a consummate capitalist even as I railed against bureaucracy and greed). I returned damaged goods— even spoiled milk—to stores, held onto warranties, called the cops on neighbors who refused to silence their dogs' late-night barking, denounced women's exploitation in the fields of teaching and publishing, challenged my status and salary at work (by ensuring that my position, no longer merely secretarial, was reclassified). It would seem, on the surface, that I was a master of asserting myself: I had even been asked to lead an assertiveness-training workshop for college students, primarily women.

But so much of my letter writing, manager hating, and hand wringing was basically self-destructive. To borrow Emily Dickinson's words, "I aimed my Pebble—but Myself / Was all the one that fell." I couldn't sleep at night for the angers that seethed within me; my preliminary businesslike requests were soon followed by demands and tears. I could neither accept nor ignore the noises next door. It seems to me now that like the children who haven't language for their abusers and abuse, but who nonetheless, according to child psychologists, "tell," I had been acting out what I felt to be the abusive dimensions of being a woman/consumer/alienated worker in western society. But like many of these children's parents and social workers, no one "heard."[4]

I was a parody of the diligent homemaker; because I wasn't in a position to bake, can, quilt, garden, or even home-decorate, I shopped for bargains and tried to perform, through consumer activism, what I took to be my material duties as a grown-up woman. While I might eventually receive an apology from a mail-order house or obtain the petition I needed three other annoyed neighbors to sign against the offending one, I had no real power, and the military-industrial complex as well as male neighbors with Doberman pinschers and red Corvettes—which (or whom) I somehow link together—would do damage again, not only to me.

I thought if I were trained and accredited in the law, I would have power over all my harassers. I didn't know that such power eludes even women attorneys or, more importantly, that attempts to overpower another are nothing if not self-destructive. Moreover, I didn't see what Griffin does, that "the culture which educates me and whose language I speak wants to silence women" (*MFE* 186). At the law symposium, I had glowed with pride as my group asked whether I was already a law student, intimating that I should be, that I spoke like a lawyer, and so forth. I was proud, too, subsequently, when I was accepted into that conservative, prestigious law school after, I thought, proving once again my linguistic powers (and the power of language) on the entrance exam and essay.

Clearly I hadn't yet read and recognized Audre Lorde's conviction that "*the master's tools will never dismantle the master's house*" (*Sister Outsider* 112). When I did read Lorde's essay I questioned the logic of her image while relishing its rhetorical ring: Why can't the master's tools dismantle his house? The tools are nothing without their worker. And yet: Maybe the image isn't right, but the sentiment surely could be. In my case, my tool was language, but even harboring the notion of "mastering" language was proof that I was stuck in the "master's house." Like it or not, I was already implicated in, even a privileged member of, the "master" system. As Rich observes in *Blood, Bread, and Poetry* (1987), "White women are situated within white patriarchy as well as against it" (x). The greater the facility I had with the master's language the more I was tied to the system I considered dismantling. Once I accept the notion of a master and his tools I have bought into the old duality/hierarchy of master/slave, powerful/weak, male/female, even if I steal the tools. This hierarchical system grants power to women or others angry at their oppression only so long as they acquiesce in the perpetuating of the patriarchy.

But I was not willing to accept only the power accorded those who don't make waves, what Elizabeth Janeway calls the "power of the weak." I didn't believe that I could manage silence sweetly and subversively, or even that I could sweet-talk or street-walk my way around men, but what other alternatives to legal action and language were there? I couldn't make my way to a powerful man's heart through his stomach (nor did I want to). And I didn't have a women's group for support and Janeway's "effective action." I had only the words I worked at alone as a writer, until, that is, I read such feminist poet-critics as Cherríe Moraga, Anzaldúa, Rich, Lorde, Griffin, and Piercy, whose discursive power through creative prose forms both the subject and the inspiration for this study.

I was plagued by proliferating questions. Elizabeth Bishop would have put it:

> The acuteness of the question
> forks instantly and starts
> a snake-tongue flickering
> . . . becoming helplessly proliferative.
> ("Faustina, or, Rock Roses")

Can power be truly positive? Even what is called "power-within" (as distinguished from "power-over") can intimidate those without it. Surely some of the male academics who verbally intimidated me specifically tried not to do so, but it happened anyway: Does asserting the self necessarily mean denying another? Can parachuting away from one kind of discourse (closed, legal, patriarchal, academic, impersonal, elitist) to another (open, revolutionary, feminist, quotidian, personal) solve such a problem? Is it possible to write and speak differently, after all? And if so, would we still (or finally!) get published? Would we be heard? Would we lose our jobs, be denied tenure? Where would the difference(s) reside—in new genres, new grammar, new voices, new imagery? The American poet-critics I read answer or continue to ask these questions in many ways.

Rich determinedly rewrites the very definition of *power* in *Blood, Bread, and Poetry:*

> The word *power* is highly charged for women. It has been long associated with the use of force, with rape, with the stockpiling of weapons, with the ruthless accrual of wealth and the hoarding of resources, with the power that acts only in its own interest, despising and exploiting the powerless—including women and children. The effects of this kind of power are all around us, even literally in the water we drink and the air we breathe, in the form of carcinogens and radioactive wastes. But for a long time now, feminists have been talking about redefining power, about that meaning of power which returns to the root . . . to be able, to have the potential, to possess and use one's energy of creation—*transforming power.* (5)

Like Rich, Anzaldúa also clearly believes creative power, which is indispensable, is tied up in personal power: "A lack of belief in my creative self, is a lack of belief in my total self and vice versa—I cannot separate my writing from any part of my life. It is all one" (73). Both Rich and she imply that power of a certain sort ("transforming," "creative") is both good and separate from exploitative kinds of power. They echo other feminists like Nancy Hartsock, who in 1981 wrote: "A feminist definition of power—power as energy, effective interaction, or empowerment—contrasts with and challenges the assumption of power as domination or control" (quoted in Thorne, Kramarae, Henley 19).

Janeway suggests that too often women are kept down by their fears of reinforcing the power system and that perhaps they should dismiss such questions as: "Suppose I make a breakthrough; what will I get that's worth the hassle? Won't I have to commit myself to masculine goals and techniques for doing my work that I both dislike and resent, personally and in principle? How can a woman get anywhere without following Henry Higgins's suggestion and being more like a man? Do I want to pay that price in order to lay my hands on power? In fact, do I really want to lay my hands on it at all?" (326). But I can't afford to dismiss the question of being assimilated or co-opted, positioned as I am in the academy. I agree with Rich's assertion in "Teaching Language in Open Admissions" that "at the bedrock level of my thinking . . . is the sense that language is power. . . . But this notion hangs on a special conception of what it means to be released into language: *not simply learning the jargon of an elite, fitting unexceptionably into the status quo,* but learning that language can be used as a means of changing reality" (*LSS* 67; emphasis mine). But often Rich herself (as here or in her redefinition of *power*) writes in a top-down hierarchical manner, proving *A* is better than *B,* perhaps deploying the "jargon of the elite" against which she speaks. Is her "dream of a common language" just a dream? Or can we, by a commitment to writing of our own experience, making the professional personal (as Sandra Gilbert maintains feminist critics do), reach academic and nonacademic audiences alike?

I had felt great relief when I read Rich's ideas and the common yet nonconventional forms and ideas of such authors as Griffin, Anzaldúa, Lorde, Moraga, Russ, Judy Grahn, Alice Walker, Louise Bernikow, and so many other poet-critics. I felt I had finally uncovered a language and history (not only for the physical harassment but for the extremely efficient if not obvious silencing I'd experienced for years). But almost immediately I was told, by those concerned for my academic welfare or by the examples of those who were not, not to write like them. My critics and protectors realized, with Tompkins, that "to break with conventions is to risk not being heard at all" ("Me and My Shadow" 171). English feminist Michelene Wandor, who writes in a variety of genres, sometimes in the same work, admits she feels, "a continual uncertainty that [her] voice may not be heard, because it does not run smoothly into any single, clear channel" (86).

And yet I speak of these matters because now I do believe powerful—because unconventional—feminist discourse is possible. If Rich writes what might be called hardheaded, logical prose, she also relies on personal narrative, confession, and anecdote to counter masculinist values and forms, as a "means of changing reality." And in other ways, other texts, Rich has fully broken with academic conventions. I think of the present-tense, autobiographical frame to her essay on Emily Dickinson, and I think of her book *Of Woman Born: Motherhood as Experience and Institution* (1976), a work emphatically weaving autobiography with sermon and documentary, research and polemic. As Marge Piercy describes the latter work:

> *Of Woman Born* is not primarily a scholarly work. It proceeds in dolphin leaps and dives. It arches into the air of facts, history, anthropology, political annals, arguing as it goes. It dives far down into the painful dark regions of Adrienne Rich's own buried experience as the mother of three sons, as wife, as daughter, her guilt and rage and confusion and sense of betrayal. It is alternately dry and wet, reasoned and impassioned, analytical and intuitive. . . . I am sure the book has been attacked because it is a profoundly feminist book in idea and argument and impact. But I am equally sure it has been attacked because the form of the book itself is the product of feminist discipline. (*PCB* 269)

Rich and those others I have mentioned inspire other women to write in their own voices ("follow your own path; it's okay to do that," Rich said at the 1988 University of Washington Roethke Memorial Reading).

I speak of these matters in an academic context (the question of tenure, the law school symposium, the harassing professors) because that is where I find myself and where at least some of these questions about language are being discussed. Moreover, I speak of these matters in the manner of a story because women may well have different ways of knowing—that is, through narrative—than men.[5] The narrative or testimonial mode is one of those features of feminist essays I find personally indispensable. In fact, I mean to argue throughout that feminist critics' reliance on narrative, testimony, anecdote, poetry—on a self-conscious mixture or patchwork of genres—is one powerful way of re-vising the conventional academic modes they would criticize. Barbara Christian asserts that people of color have always theorized "in forms quite different from the Western form of abstract logic . . . often in narrative forms, in . . . stories" (336). In part these writers project onto and into the aesthetic realm the barriers they sense in their emotional, familial, economic, professional, and political lives. By pushing against perceived (even if not always actually rigid) generic and literary boundaries, cross-genre writers try to translate and traverse borders usually considered more "real" and material than literary.

I am a little worried about having presented some professors in a negative light; I'm plagued by the good-girl formulas fed me all the years. I think of Marge Piercy, who writes of the censor inside:

> The censor says, you can't say that, it will hurt your mother/ father/brother/sister/husband/wife/lover/child/friend. The censor says, write that and you'll lose that promotion or even your job or you'll lose custody of your kids. The censor says, What will your comrades say about that one? Is that politically correct according to the slogan-of-the-month club? The censor says, are you going to admit that in public? Nobody will want to sleep with you. Nobody will like you anymore. They'll laugh at you behind your back. The censor says, That sounds crazy. (*PCB* 55)

I think of Susan Griffin, who confesses, "All the time I wrote that book [*Woman and Nature*], the patriarchal voice was in me (the way the voice of order whispers to me now) that I had no proof for any of my writing, that I was wildly in error, that the vision I had of the whole work was absurd" (*MFE* 231). Yet, as Griffin writes elsewhere, "To speak, to write, and act out of one's own experience is a radical idea, but it is not new" (*MFE* 5).

I must dare to speak out, even against the professorial clan, in order to convey a truth: that in a way all professors, given the inevitable power disparity in academia, are harassers, including those females long praised and rewarded for thinking like men. I reason on analogy with the case of the mentally disturbed woman who thought her kind father meant to kill her; her therapist knew she was wrong, literally speaking, yet the patient was also right about his—and society's—relation to her: it was a killing one.[6] I speak of these matters because I will continue writing out of my experience as I speak about, in the course of these chapters, other writers, accomplished hands at writing and acting out of their own experiences as women. Obviously, something happened between the time I was accepted to law school and this writing. I deliberated long about leaving a job I liked—helping administer a university writing program—to learn instead legal language and go into deep debt. I formally deferred my admission for a year as I thought about where I could best be (or perhaps re-construct) myself.

Rich has lectured, "Refuse to give up your capacity to think as a woman, even though in graduate school and professions . . . you will be praised and rewarded for 'thinking like a man'" (*BBP* 4–5). It finally dawned on me I might feel a bit like Mario Baeza, a graduate of the law school I would have attended, initially felt: "This is the system that said 'separate can be equal.' This is the system that said 'Dred Scot is property.'. . . And I did not hear the word 'justice' once" (Chapman 11).

I knew, because I had visited several classes, that I would be appalled repeatedly at the emotional and moral content lacking in legal lectures; I would miss the mere sound of (the) poetic (word) "justice." Being a law student might simply be another way of acting out the harassment I felt I was always receiving at the hands of a patriarchy. (When asked why I was applying to law school, I told several friends I felt a need to "sue everybody," certainly no solution to my general feeling of powerlessness.) Perhaps what I needed was a kind of double literacy—legal or patriarchal terms for patriarchal ills (employment discrimination, harassment, sexual assault) and institutional attempts at cures (equal-opportunity employer, no-fraternizing clauses, comparable worth, welfare) as well as woman-centered words of personal experience and re-vision. But I was most desperate for the latter.

I too had been a poet, though it was doubtful if in my on-

going self-doubt I still was, yet I was still making my own coin-
ages in stolen moments, without much recognition (which to me
meant without much success), when I applied to law school. I ad-
mit that part of me wanted to prove to my former classmates
that I was not merely a poet (in their minds, an apolitical, alogi-
cal anachronism). I also wanted to earn more respect and money
than that accorded academic literary specialists or writers, es-
pecially those without a teaching appointment. I wanted to
merge the creative writer and the intellectual, the dreamer and
the doer. I had been hurt by all the law-school-bound men I knew
in college who habitually had excluded me from their farm-
worker/social-democratic/Marxist dialogues and diatribes. I re-
call being both angry and cheered when I read what I took to
be a description of my plight in Piercy's poem "In the Men's
Room(s)":

In the Men's Room(s)

When I was young I believed in intellectual
  conversation:
I thought the patterns we wove on stale smoke
floated off to the heaven of ideas.
To be certified worthy of high masculine discourse
like a potato grater I would rub on contempt,
suck snubs, wade proudly through the brown stuff on the
  floor.
They were talking of integrity and existential ennui
while the women ran out for six-packs and had abortions
in the kitchen and fed the children and were auctioned
  off.
Eventually of course I learned how their eyes perceived
  me:
when I bore to them cupped in my hands a new poem to
  nibble,
when I brought my aerial maps of Sartre or Marx,
they said, she is trying to attract our attention,
she is offering up her breasts and thighs.
I walked on eggs, their tremulous equal:
they saw a fish peddler hawking in the street.

Now I get coarse when the abstract nouns start flashing.
I go out to the kitchen and talk cabbages and habits.
I try hard to remember to watch what people do.
Yes, keep your eyes on the hands, let the voice go
    buzzing.
Economy is the bone, politics is the flesh,
watch who they beat and who they eat,
watch who they relieve themselves on, watch who they
    own.
The rest is decoration.
(*COW* 80)

With such women's wisdom in my ears, I convinced myself I would be truer to myself—and the language around me would be truer to my experience—if I put off enrolling in law school and applied to doctoral programs in literature instead. But it seems another one of my motivations for applying to law school had been a desire to prove I could compete at that which was a conventional task for a middle-class Jew: going to professional school. I had proven I could compete.

Yet such a privileged attitude makes me wonder: How could I have been afraid that law school would mold me into a member of the ruling class when I was so clearly a person of privilege before I'd even been admitted? How could I remove the blinders my privileged upbringing brought me and instead seek what Rich calls "a common language" (for Judy Grahn's "common woman")?[7] How could Rich? We both grew up the daughters of Jewish doctors and gentile mothers, were Ivy League–educated, wrote poems, married young and ultimately unsuccessfully. Unlike me, she is a mother, lesbian, and a widely recognized public figure, but we both share ties and tension with the father, his laws, and language. We share the urge to forge new forms and new communities. We both weave from poetry to prose.

These many years later, I feel far more empowered by feminist poet-critics than I imagine I could ever have been by law school. Their alchemizing their lives into poems and prose, admitting as they do their inner conflicts and contradictions, inspires me to do the same, to respond in kind to their words, to try to frame my experience poetically, narratively, unabashedly, to find alternatives to both legal and strictly academic utterance. To be a creative, not co-opted, critic.

Having passable memories of obtaining two masters' degrees (one in teaching writing, one in writing poetry), I hoped that when I came to the University of Washington for a Ph.D. I could learn how women poets can change the master discourse(s) of academic writing, a discourse that, oppressive as it was, is nonetheless more open than the law to revision. How radically it can be revised and whether I wanted to be that radical were open questions, ones I continue to address at Skidmore College, where I now teach. Luckily, many women writers and even some early (mostly male) poet-critics and several poststructuralist, reader-response, and composition theorists had paved the way for my writing and reading differently.

Robert Von Hallberg claims that American poet-critics since 1945 are more direct about stating premises than academic critics, and that for them criticism is an "improvisatory art, unpredictable, full of inconsistencies" (286–88). And Helen Vendler explains that "because logic—the system of divisibility—voiced itself as the Law in school, it became for [Roland] Barthes the symbol of patriarchy, violence, the father, while intermixture became the symbol of the mother and of the aesthetic" ("The Medley Is the Message," *Music* 60). Houston Baker speaks of space being opened for personal poetry in the critical field, and calls his criticism a personal project. Certainly French writers Hélène Cixous and Luce Irigaray experiment with different voices, parody and paraphrase, poetry and abstraction.[8] But it is the journeys and journalizing of contemporary American feminist mixed-genre writers I want most to join. It is they who are most confiding of their compositional methods, their lives, their relation to language. Metadiscursive, autobiographical, familiar, they invite readers into conversation, emulation. They are less interested in the merely experimental than the experiential.

When I was in college I would write poems around the edges of my days, at a precarious slant-top desk. I wrote most when I was most pressured with conventional academic tasks—term papers, exams, heavy reading. It occurs to me that I've always been drawn to and productive in the margins, as writers like Cherríe Moraga and Gloria Anzaldúa are at their best writing about and from the "borderlands." So I'm torn between wishing to argue for a new centrality or predominance of the autobiographical, mixed-genre mode and simply speaking about and from it, presenting it in situ. The fact of the matter is, although Jean Kennard was probably right when she wrote in 1981 that "most feminist critics, . . . though often willing to discuss a wider range of material beyond the text, nevertheless write from the objective stance of the New Critics" ("Personally Speaking" 142), there are now far more feminist critics practicing what they preach, that is, writing differently. I intend, therefore, to discuss as many of these empowering and empowered writers as I can.

By not relegating these self-disclosures and the purposes of my project to a preface, I mean to signal my collaboration with writers who dream of bridging private and public discourse, lives and letters. Tompkins summarizes well what I've been working toward during these years in Seattle and Saratoga. She writes, "The criticism I would like to write would always take off from personal experience, would always be in some way a chronicle of my hours and days, would speak in a voice which can talk about everything, would reach out to a reader like me and touch me where I want to be touched" ("Me and My Shadow" 173). I believe very deeply in practicing (as in rehearsing as well as carrying out) a feminist aesthetic of personal responses to literature—and to my literary education. Diverse as contemporary feminist poet-critics may be, they all presuppose that liberation from patriarchal values and practices must take place, if not begin, in language itself. My models are those feminists whose writing embodies the refusals, revisions, fluidities, alchemies, collages, quilts, gardens, border crossings, cross-hatchings about which they speak. Their *essais,* like my own, try, experiment with, make forays into different genres, sashaying into the world of academic rhetoric and back out again, making and registering changes and challenges as they go.

Since Adrienne Rich is perhaps the exemplary contemporary American cross-genre feminist critic, it is no surprise that many of the issues I explore are essentialized in poems like the one I quote as an epigraph to this chapter, "Power" (1974):

Living   in the earth-deposits   of our history

Today a backhoe divulged   out of a crumbling flank of earth
one bottle   amber   perfect   a hundred-year-old
cure for fever   or melancholy   a tonic
for living on this earth   in the winters of this climate

Today I was reading about Marie Curie:
she must have known she suffered   from radiation sickness
her body bombarded for years   by the element
she had purified
It seems she denied to the end
the source of the cataracts on her eyes
the cracked and suppurating skin   of her finger-ends
till she could no longer hold   a test-tube or a pencil

She died   a famous woman   denying
her wounds
denying
her wounds   came   from the same source as her power.
(*FD* 225)

In this poem describing the life and death of atomic scientist Marie Curie, Rich implies that women "master" or work with the father's laboratory (or language) at the risk of our own annihilation and, worse, at the risk of our complicity with that fact. Curie "denied" both her wounds and her antagonist(s)—radium, fame, a culture seeking bombs. Thus, her life allegorizes that of many women: she gained power from sources that could and would kill her. Radium and the search for (its) power blinded her; radium caused both cataracts and cancer. The more famous she became, the more deadly grams of radium she received in tribute. Curie's "masculine" mode of behavior, "denying her wounds," is a failed survival—and writing—strategy. If history doesn't bury us, our denial of our own history does, Rich suggests. Thus language, like radium, can empower and destroy, however much women might like to deny it.

When I learned the term *sexual harassment,* I was both empowered to stop the harasser and endangered by the fact that the system has so accommodated the act that it gives it a name. The act is tamed (its individual variations are flattened out while the conditions for its occurrence are far from eradicated) even as it is singled out as a crime. Similarly, when a woman becomes Mrs. Smith, she becomes not somebody but a thing, property of Mr. Smith. Though she now (at least in the U.S. in this century) assumes legal right to Mr. Smith's home and property (or theirs), she has destroyed in some ways her old, at least potentially autonomous, self. By seeking new critical language and forms, feminist critics hope to circumvent women's erasure.

On the other hand, though Rich elsewhere notes that "old language is [not] good enough for our descriptions of the world we are trying to transform," she nonetheless posits "the oppressor's language" as better than "lies, secrets, and silence": "this is the oppressor's language / yet I need it to talk to you" ("The Burning of Paper Instead of Children," *FD* 117). Sometimes the "old language" is transformative enough to have seen oppression at work: "what we *see,* we *see* / and *seeing* is changing," Rich writes in another poem, "Planetarium" (*FD* 115; emphasis mine); she is not blinded as Curie was. Moreover, by musing and writing on women like Curie, creating poetry that "divulges" rather than denies the facts of a woman's life and death, Rich counters the silence and denial that were so deadly for Curie. Speaking out, telling one's story, in whatever voice one might have, is a matter of survival for women.

A poem itself may be seen as folk medicine, capable of ancient alchemy and miracle cures, opposed to male-identified science. In "Power," "a backhoe divulged   out of a crumbling flank of earth / one bottle   amber   perfect   a hundred-year-old / cure for fever   or melancholy   a tonic." Rich similarly unearths Marie Curie's history, offers us a tonic, the poem, as compensation for the past, as hope or incentive for change or cure. While Curie, unfortunately, cannot be cured by such an imagined tonic, the "divulged" bottle, something no longer concealed, symbolizes the curative effect an admission of past injury and compassion for a foremother can have on others. Writing her poem, Rich makes a tonic out of Curie's past suffering; she suggests readers counter denial with a heavy dose of the truth about the past and their own present. Reciting not just poems but "our history" can both reveal and heal wounds.

When I first read "Power," I thought it suggested creative power comes from pain, that not only is the poet sage and physician, as Keats maintained, but that the poems derive from the pain they intend to cure. Now, however, I believe less that the poet herself has to seek out pain and poverty, for example, though she may seek to give solace to others for their troubles.

But there is a paradox at work in the poem (as there is in the title of this chapter).[9] While her poem argues for an aesthetic, a praxis, of speaking out about one's perils (and thus rejects both the macho stance of working unflinchingly for fame and progress in the face of personal disaster and the stereotypical feminine stance of denying one's needs and ills—"Don't worry about little ole me, Dear"), Rich only later begins to speak comfortably in the first person, autobiographically. She first had to acknowledge that she had achieved poetic success by publishing poems that denied both her gender and the problems she suffered as a woman in a patriarchy. In her 1982 poem "Sources," Rich says "It is only now, under a powerful womanly lens, that I can decipher your suffering and deny no part of my own" (*Sources* 15). She is not speaking about Curie, but about her father, yet the quote is nonetheless apt: only over time could Rich come to express directly in her writing her own suffering.

In her first book of collected prose, *On Lies, Secrets, and Silence* (1978), Rich apologizes for "using [herself] as an illustration" in her 1971 essay "When We Dead Awaken: Writing as Re-Vision" (38). By 1984, when she reissues some of her work, she is adding apologies for old practices: "In 1953, when ['The Tourist and the Town'] was written, a notion of male experience as universal prevailed which made the feminine pronoun suspect, or merely 'personal.' In this poem, as in 'Afterward,' I later altered the pronouns [made them feminine] because they alter, for me, the dimensions of the poem" (*FD* 329).

Perhaps one way we begin to speak out for ourselves is to speak out for others (or about other poets), as Rich has. Curie (like Anne Bradstreet, Jane Austen, and Virginia Woolf, some of the subjects of Rich's first book of collected essays) is a "find" like the tonic bottle "divulged" in the first stanza of "Power." Rich's alchemical power to make a woman's life—Curie's, her own—into a poem is a good kind of power, a power ascribed to folk medicine and opposed to, for example, nuclear power. Women critics writing on lost or undervalued writers set the stage for their own reclamation and self-assertion. Thus, feminist criticism can be seen as having moved, somewhat in concert with other modern criticisms, from a focus on texts to a focus on readers—and a focus on readers as writers, as well.

One of the limits of a poem like "Power," however, is its size; like the sonnet, it circumscribes.[10] Lyric poems, like the jewel-like but also down-to-earth amber bottle in "Power," preserve bits of the past; they fail, however, to do what the epic attempts to: that is, incorporate a large-scale view of history.[11] Traditional lyrics create the illusion of a speaker being overheard confiding private matters to self or God; the reader is let in on the story as if by accident. Traditional epics depend on battles, male superheroes, and formal, ceremonial rhetoric for their depiction of history. Often the lyric, and certainly the epic, cannot accommodate the woman wishing to connect overtly with a listener or reader as well as join the private and public views of history, not to mention accomplish this in common language.

She may need to stretch the boundaries of traditional forms, as some feminist critics maintain she stretches the boundaries of her ego.[12] In keeping with a female tradition of making do with limited (material) means, of writing in stolen moments, in patches, writers of the contemporary literary criticism described in this study weave autobiography into history and criticism, poetry into prose, journal into analysis. Moreover, they allow the seams of such cross-genre work to show; they celebrate and announce their need and capacity for alchemy. As Suzanne Juhasz details:

> Recently, feminist writers, *consciously seeking forms more appropriate to the truth of their experience as women,* have seen the connection between the shape of their lives and the shape of habitual writing by women, like the journal. In addition, they have seen the traditional social barrier between the public and private worlds as not only sexist but artificial. Works as varied as Adrienne Rich's *Of Woman Born* . . . Susan Griffin's *Woman and Nature,* and Louise Bernikow's *Among Women* all grant validity and significance to private, personal experience, rather than trying to 'transcend' it. All seek formal equivalents for their inclusion of the private worlds in a public document. ("Journal as Source" 17; emphasis mine)

Many of Rich's prose works begin, like her poem "Power," with a written text and take off from there as they weave a crosshatch of autobiography, quasi-conventional literary criticism, and, occasionally, poetry. In her foreword to *On Lies, Secrets, and Silence,* in fact, Rich denounces the denial and "muffl[ing] in silence over and over" of the entire history of women's struggle for self-determination; she asks women to rely (as she does in "Power") on past life stories, past texts. So Rich begins her collection of essays with "The Tensions of Anne Bradstreet" and in each subsequent essay makes reference to informing or disturbing works. It is in the prefaces to these essays that first-person autobiographical bits of manifesto loom largest, but even in the second essay of the collection, "When We Dead Awaken: Writing as Re-Vision," there is the characteristic move from text to published text to Rich's own: "In rereading Virginia Woolf's *A Room of One's Own* (1929) . . . , I was astonished at the sense of effort, of pains taken, of dogged tentativeness, in the tone of that essay. And I recognized that tone. I had heard it often enough, in myself and in other women. It is the tone of a woman almost in touch with her anger, who is determined not to appear angry, who is *willing* herself to be calm, detached, and even charming in a roomful of men where things have been said which are attacks on her very integrity" (37). Although on the very next page Rich confesses that she hesitates to do what she's "about to do now, which is to use [herself] as an illustration" (38), she has clearly already begun to speak of herself unapologetically ("I recognized that tone. I had heard it often enough, in myself"). In fact, Rich authorizes the use of the first person, if without quite realizing it, by asserting that "self-knowledge, for women, is more than a search for identity: it is part of our refusal of the self-destructiveness of male-dominated society" (35). This assertion resonates with the message I read in "Power": To know the self we must speak of and from it. We must refuse to be accomplices in our own self-destruction. We must refuse or renounce silence and denial.

Yet women seeking alternatives to male-dominated discourse worry that the very anomalousness of their writing will keep them from being heard. With respect to weaving autobiography into criticism, Rich asserts, "It's a lot easier and less dangerous to talk about other women writers" (38). Michelene Wandor knows that her "wide and wild and sometimes varied" voices make it hard for her to be catalogued by publishers, critics, readers (86). These women writers want their voices, wild by traditional standards, but familiar to many women, published so the common woman can hear them. Each writer becomes more comfortable and more accessible the more she makes such self-disclosing statements as these, especially in prose.

If their poetry, despite such promising titles as *The Dream of a Common Language* or *The Work of a Common Woman,* is still deemed difficult and inaccessible by "common woman" readers (as opposed to traditional critics or publishers), writers such as Rich and Grahn do well to switch at least occasionally to prose. In prose they may get closest to the commonest writing by women. They can employ what has become a tradition in women's studies—the interdisciplinary mode—as a structuring device in their writing. They can cross the borders between disciplinary discourses as well as the traditional borders between the writer and reader and the writer and her subject. They can discover what Annie Dillard found (or asserted) for herself in literary nonfiction: "There's nothing you cannot do with it. No subject matter is forbidden. No structure is proscribed. You get to make up your own form every time" (74).

In her "Toward a More Feminist Criticism" (*BBP*), Rich does try to prescribe some ways in which the feminist critic can get the most out of her form and the privilege of her being able to write at all. But she does not mean to define one "correct line." She calls for more writing from women "who will test the work against their experience—who, like Woolf's 'common reader,' are interested in literature as a key to life, not an escape from it" (91). Rich talks about two kinds of feminist criticism being written, one kind published in journals and the other in magazines. Rich's own essay, however, gives the lie to the split: she writes, and writes here, for both kinds of audiences. She asks that the feminist critic be "as clear as possible about the compromises she makes, about her own fear and trembling as she sits down to write; to admit her limitations when she picks up work by women who write from a very different culture" (95), as she herself so often tries to do.

She asks us to share in the power of each other's work and to call "into question most of the activity of the dominant lit. crit. and the culture it reflects" (99). She hopes that "feminist criticism can renounce the temptation to be graceful, pleasing, and respectable and strive instead to be strong-minded, rash, and dangerous" (99). While some feminist critics may strive to be recuperative rather than dangerous, all of the feminist critics I have mentioned so far share common themes: renouncing the self-denial implicit in the old language(s) of criticism and gaining the power present in writing the self—naming rather than denying both our wounds and the nature of our powers. These themes are articulated repeatedly, from Olsen's observation that "every woman who writes is a survivor" (which is itself quoted in Rich, *LSS* 256), to Rich's comment that Grahn's original "Common Woman" sequence is a study in "power and powerlessness" (*LSS* 255–56). The difficulty is, as Rich points out in "Transcendental Etude,"

No one ever told us we had to study our lives,
make of our lives a study, as if learning natural history
or music. . . .
(*FD* 265)

TWO

Border Crossing as Method and Motif in Contemporary Feminist Writing

[Autobiography is the] simplest of literary enterprises and commonest, without rules or formal requirements. . . . Here all sorts of generic boundaries (and even lines dividing discipline from discipline) are simply wiped away, and we often cannot tell whether we should call something a novel, a poem, a critical dissertation, or an autobiography.

James Olney, "Autobiography and the Critical Moment" (1980)

[Freud] too worked at the juncture of the autobiographical and the theoretical, inventing a science by interpreting his own dreams and personal history in connection with his work with others. . . . Willy-nilly, he stumbled into a realm of knowledge where science is not clearly separated from poetry.

Jane Gallop, *Thinking Through the Body* (1988)

When as a sophomore English major I learned that several of my professors considered Freud's and other psychoanalysts' writing relevant to the study of literature, I looked around my father's collection for a book of Freud's work. I knew my father had once intended to become a psychiatrist and had earned an M.A. in psychology; moreover, he had an extensive collection of books, most stamped with the little man (Mercury) that is the logo of the Random House "Modern Library." The text I found, *The Basic Writings of Sigmund Freud,* translated, edited, and introduced by Dr. A. A. Brill, fascinated me, and my father said I could keep it for my own. I have it to this day, though I have not read much beyond Brill's introduction, having taken most of my Freud in smaller, paperback doses doctored by other editors and translators. But what fascinated me about this edition was the final footnote to Brill's introduction, "Alas! As these pages are going to the printer we have been startled by the terrible news that the Nazi holocaust has suddenly encircled Vienna and that Professor Freud and his family are virtual prisoners in the hands of civilization's greatest scourge" (32). This footnote showed me that a book's "borders"—its packaging, format, and the contexts in which it is read and published—are inseparable from its more apparent content. Not only was an author more a part of the text than I had imagined, but so were its editors and readers. Brill alerted me to the fact that every book, every reading, is laced and surrounded with circumstances worth considering, border crossings within the text as well as at its edges. (It wasn't until later that I saw the sustained and sophisticated use of border imagery foregrounded in works by ethnic-American women.)

Brill's entire introduction expresses, even without its final alarm and news brief, such personal and dramatic concern for the safekeeping of Freud's works that I was shocked, since such voicings, such extratextual paraphernalia, were not a concern of the New Criticism practiced in the literature seminars of my day. The introduction forced me to be an active reader newly attentive to the many forces behind a published text. I was intrigued by Brill's personal relationships with Freud and Jung as well as with the notion that Nazism threatened all readers of the Random House *Basic Writings* along with "Professor Freud." I was amazed by the intrusion of the "real" world into the written. I might never read another book immune to the circumstances of its production and my reception. For all I could not comprehend the bulk of the translated Freud, I nonetheless could be both moved and amused by Brill's old-fashioned cry, "Alas!"

Knowing little about Freud at the time, I had no idea whether he escaped the Nazi occupation unharmed or died in fear or violence. World War II became suddenly real to me, while Freud's life became novelistic: he, his translators, and I traversed the borders of fiction and fact, story and data. I felt invaded by the text as my personal circumstances seemed suddenly written into it. Brill couldn't resist the simultaneous melodrama and authenticity of an exclamatory footnote; I couldn't resist it either—as this writing, with its occasional deliberate archaisms, demonstrates. Furthermore, the text expanded to include for me the mysterious fact of my father the doctor almost becoming a psychiatrist; my own desire for father Freud's book from my father's large library of male-tattooed texts; my being a woman with a Jewish surname long after the Nazi reign and Freud's death from natural causes; and, finally, my written record of all this here. We were language lovers all—writer, translator, reader. Philology brought us into countries occupied by one another. Footnotes, margin notes suddenly confettied and confounded the tome.

Like my father, however, I am not a psychoanalyst, so I will stop the story, whose full psychological significance is likely beyond me, here. I can say, though, that in the footnote (or this preamble) lies the beginning of my fascination with texts on the border, authors in war zones, the imagery of edges, cross fire, cross-hatching. Yet I wanted my own library, one of recent writers whose experiences were closer to my own, one with no more little men embossing the book covers. Perhaps even more to the point, I needed to tell my own story, and now I am. As Barbara Christian, quoting Marcelle Thiébaux, writes in *Black Feminist Criticism,* "The only possible library for a woman is one invented by herself, writing herself or her own discourse into it" (x).

When I began to write poems, I found it necessary to express what I considered the endpoints of my identity: the Russian

Jew and the Ukrainian Catholic. Part of what disturbed me about the Freudian footnote was that I was a Jew terrified of Nazism, and yet I was not a Jew. I felt awed and guilty as I read about Freud's danger: I was not a Jew in danger; I didn't know enough about World War II; I felt *ineligible* to learn even my own family's history. I wrote poems informed by these twin senses of uncertainty and guilt, and learned that my identity was not in fact neatly suspended between two poles or endpoints. Instead, like the identities of the ethnic-American women whose border-crossing works also inform this chapter,[1] my identity oscillates among sometimes fogged-in points of reference, multiple angles of vision—and confusion. Like these contemporary poet-critics, I find I oscillate between poetry and prose as well. I seek prose to relieve the gnomic anxiety of poetry, poetry to override the seeming clarity and control of prose. Prose has tidy borders on the page, poetry a tidal edge— no clear edge at all.

Though poetry may "speak the language of wildness and danger," it is also, according to Susan Griffin, "a secret way through which we can restore authenticity to ourselves" (*MFE* 245). Alternating prose with poetry keeps me from sticking too blandly to a critical discourse I find constricting, helps me find my true subject and subjectivity, as the Lacanians say. And that subjectivity is inevitably crosshatched, multiple.

In my poems "The Performance" and "The Way the Gravestones Align," I cross and examine (or cross-examine) the borders, edges, limits, overlaps of my ethnic and religious identities. Like Adrienne Rich, I grew up technically neither Jew nor Gentile and yet temperamentally, genealogically, both. Under Conservative or Orthodox Jewish law, Rich and I are not Jewish because our mothers are not. We also do not qualify under Reformed Jewish law because although one parent was Jewish, we were not raised as Jews.[2] And I'm not considered Catholic because my father is not, although my having been baptized may complicate things.

While Rich had a largely Christian social life and even attended for five years an Episcopalian church where she was baptized and confirmed, I had a largely Jewish social life in my Long Island, New York, hometown of Jericho, but I was sent to neither temple nor church and was kept fairly ignorant of both religions, their rituals, their politics. I did learn that my mother's church had been a Ukrainian Catholic one, itself a cross between the Greek and Russian Orthodox churches, though the services in her hometown, Shamokin, Pennsylvania, were in either Latin or Ukrainian. When I was about eight, I found a rosary in her bedroom and I asked her whether she still believed in Jesus; she said yes. And then, about the time I was twelve and beginning to attend my school friends' bar or bat mitzvahs, my mother told me I had been baptized as an infant and that I had godparents somewhere in Pennsylvania. My younger sisters and brother had not been similarly baptized, and I never saw my godparents. I was left in limbo, which alternately relieved me (I did not have to learn Hebrew like my complaining friends, nor did I have to devote Sundays to dressing up and quieting down) and left me painfully without faith—in anything:

The Performance

You go over the parts of your costume:
black tights, black slippers, tunic,
black cross on black string.

You wash the tights, your cap,
and your feet. You're not sure
about this part.

You play a nun, a barmaid, a singer
rolled into one.
The curtain is black, the stage dark.
They'll be filming you with eely black film.

In the dressing room, before the show,
the cast has forgotten roses.
The forgotten director has penned notes:
in yours, black squiggles say, Hold onto your
cross! (She doesn't want your arms
to bounce up and down
when you sing.)

You can do nothing right.
You've left your husband.

You forgot about gift-giving.
When you get whacked in the ass by the bartender
on stage, you don't react.
You never had any faith.
You never knew your lines.

You try to pray.

I had gotten too many mixed messages about how best to
perform, not only as an actress in an ambiguous role, but as
wife, daughter, woman, Christian, Jew. Perhaps, as Gloria An-
zaldúa confesses she sometimes feels, "I have so internalized
the borderland conflict that . . . I feel one cancels out the other,
and [I am] zero, nothing, no one" (63). I have been at a cold and
uncomfortable cross/roads:

The Way the Gravestones Align: Ithaca, NY/Shamokin, PA

When it snows, the churchyard in Ithaca
is as clean as a salt crystal.
The pastor heaves the church-big door,
and I cover my head with a red wool hat.
Sunday makes me angry;
I wear red instead of veiling myself.
I never go to church; my mother married a Jew.

But once with my grandmother and in a purple coat,
I went to a Ukrainian service in Shamokin—
where my uncle as a child fell off the only bicycle
and broke his arm, so my mother was forbidden to try.

Since in Shamokin lavender is for
ladies' death clothes, I remember
I had to beg my mother for that coat.
My cousin and I dozed as the nuns spoke.

> (Today the churchyard in Ithaca is cold,
> and all the crosswalks are empty.)

The graveyard in Shamokin is
the highest point in town, higher
than the stripped coal hills:

old women tighten *babushkas* and hoped to be buried
in warm weather, deep, with all the people there.

It was hard, that December, seeing
my lilac-clad *Baba* in the middle of a box,
feeling forced to kiss the cross, wear black,
and pray, as snow furred the ground
and made slippery our vows and wheels.

Since writing this poem and reading accounts of others
"split at the root," I am more at home with my collective past,
feeling generally enriched by my double heritage, my connec-
tion with other Americans of mixed heritage, my connection to
"old-country" Russia. I have felt a mild but lingering guilt about
not identifying equally with my parents' different heritages,
this milder guilt replacing the uneasiness I'd felt earlier about
not knowing my past, of having it kept a secret from me. But I
have also found strength in resisting what may be the coercive
aspects of each heritage: I have always caricatured my relatives
on my mother's side as people who said "be good" and those on
my father's side as those who said "do well." I suppose I feel I've
done mostly the latter by becoming a poet-scholar, following in
the tradition of my Jewish great-great-grandfather Abraham
Benjaminson. In Russia, just before the turn of the century, he
published books of Jewish philosophy and history in which four
different speakers argue in poetry (his original form contains
six words per line, six lines per stanza). In America, my Jewish
relatives are all great students, if not writers; my own father
recited Blake and Keats to me when as a child I watched him
shave. It is easy to see how I became enamored of his library
collection, including his *Oxford Book of English Verse*—and yet
I am adverse to writing formal verse myself.

In contrast, most of my Catholic relatives today work in
blue-collar jobs. My maternal grandmother, a wonderful gar-
dener, seamstress, and cook, never learned to read either Ukrai-
nian or English; my grandfather the coal miner wasn't much of a
reader or writer, though my mother tells me he was extremely
gentle, a pacifist. Herself a college-educated nurse, my mother
read my siblings and me only Bible stories in our youth. Though

she confided to me her own love for flashlight readings of Shakespeare (over the objections of her mother, who wanted her early in bed), my mother never read us poems or plays. Yet the enduring details of their lives—my aunt still lives in the house where she and my mother were born—held me too. I learned from them the pleasures of personal history and continuity in the face of my perceived conflicts and discontinuities. I grew proud of both my heritages, envious of *Baba*'s enduring faith, her girlhood in the Ukrainian countryside, and her house in the Pennsylvania hills (Long Island is flat, our house on a dull, suburban grid), if more comfortable with the Jewish intellectual tradition and the reading and writing it has led me to do.

*

Living in a state of psychic unrest, in a Borderland, is what makes poets write and artists create. . . . [A Mestiza] is subjected to a swamping of her psychological boundaries.
Gloria Anzaldúa, *Borderlands/La Frontera* (1987)

Throughout women's lives, the self is defined through social relationships; issues of fusion and merger of the self with others are significant, and ego and body boundaries remain flexible.
Judith Kegan Gardiner, "On Female Identity and Writing by Women" (1982)

As a graduate student in English, I became fascinated by post-Freudian theories like those informing Judith Kegan Gardiner's essay "On Female Identity and Writing by Women." As I came across more and more personal criticism by women, it struck me too that for women there is a "continual crossing of self and other." Because of this ego crossing or merging, Gardiner asserts, "women's writing [or reading] may blur public and private and defy completion"; it resists tidy alignment with a single genre or realm of discourse. For women, borders—of ego, genre, in some cases geography—are made to be crossed (for warring men, too, though their deadly border wars that simply reaffirm or rearrange dividing lines among nations are not what women writers seek). Gardiner notes that one manifestation of this border-crossing tendency is the autobiographical critical essay as practiced by Virginia Woolf, Adrienne Rich, Louise Bernikow, Carolyn Heilbrun, and others. For these writers, "the implied relationship between the self and what one reads and writes is personal and intense" (185).[3]

Women's "border campaigns" are thus waged textually. As I note in chapter 1, Thomas Farrell describes a "female mode," which is practiced by some men as well as by women, that at times obfuscates the boundary between the self of the author and the subject of the discourse as well as between the self and the audience (910); clearly, border crossing can be a compositional mode as well as an explicit thematic motif. To avoid monolithic monotony, to express a many-layered identity more adequately, or to achieve a closer connection with self and reader, border-crossing poet-critics may write alternately or simultaneously in multiple genres, crossing discursive boundaries even as they blur the distinctions between writer and reader, author and subject. Many women write personally in order to challenge or escape the domineering voice(s) of the male (critical) establishment(s).[4]

Feminist critics frequently express an unwillingness to dominate or alienate their readers or their subjects. Carol Ascher, Louise DeSalvo, and Sara Ruddick, collective editors of *Between Women,* perceive that women want "new types of criticism, alternate forms of cooperation . . . less compulsive, aggressive; lonely, competitive; more communal, caring, and integrated with love and politics" (xxii). In her introduction to *The New Feminist Criticism,* Elaine Showalter agrees that feminist literary critics strive to combine the theoretical and the personal (4). Feminist critics, then, are not only joining with others (being "more communal") but combining various realms that dominant society often thinks it a virtue to keep separate—the "personal" and the "theoretical," academic, or professional; or "love and politics" and "criticism," for instance. Marge Piercy too confesses she is "not able to make the distinction between the personal and the political that seems to come easily to people who have not lived their lives in struggle and group process" (*PCB* 183). Piercy suggests not only is she unable to separate herself from others, she is unable or unwilling to separate parts or aspects of herself.

Evidently, many feminist writers want intimacy and honesty with themselves along with their readers and subjects. British writer Judith Kazantis declares, "To be honest to myself, my verse must follow my life," adding, "Better still if I can write in a way which gives other people and especially women a sense of pride and closeness" (30). The goal of feminist critics, Peggy Allegro concurs, is to be "constantly . . . open to new . . . ways of making the strange familiar, new ego images, and new ways of synthesizing our private languages with each other" (184). And Susan Griffin perceives that "separated from our authentic cries we become weak imitations of who it is we think we should be" (*MFE* 249). Over and over, feminist poet-critics make explicit their methods and motives in transgressing formal conventions. Representing another way in which women writers cross borders, loop the inside to the outside, these self-disclosures themselves foster better self and group understanding.

Griffin uses the image of weaving to talk about how women move beyond the borders of their own experience, closely connecting writer to reader, speaker to hearer, creating new real-life and discursive possibilities. She notes, "Our writing, our talking, our living, our images have created another world than the man-made one we were born to, and continuously in this weaving we move, at one and the same time, toward each other, and outward, expanding the limits of the possible" (*MFE* 220). Employing another weaving/border image, Sandra Gilbert puts it this way in an interview, "For those of us who are feminist critics *and* poets there must inevitably be a seamless continuity between all the activities in which we engage" (122). Gilbert sees feminist criticism as one remedy for reviving what she sees as a lost wholeness. Piercy too writes of seamless overlaps: "A poem can momentarily heal not only the alienation of thought and feeling . . . but can fuse the different kinds of knowing and . . . weld mind back into body seamlessly" (*PCB* 20). More-over, she refers to a growing women's culture as a "great quilt for which we are stitching our own particolored blocks out of old petticoats, skirts, coats, bedsheets, blood, and berry juice" (*PCB* 299).[5]

Often such metadiscursive disclosures also explain the origins and purposes of their authors' border-crossing tropes and composition methods. For some writers, the border imagery invoked might come, as it does especially with Griffin, Gilbert, and Piercy above and in earlier American writings, from sewing, quilting, or weaving—domestic activities practiced in all the edges of the day by wives and wage-earning seamstresses alike in their societal marginality. Because quilting, for example, is often accomplished by sewing old material to new, it is akin to what Linda Anderson refers to as a woman's return to her "material origins" in the process of "becoming a subject" (59). Quilts often tell family histories, whether in scenes or symbols sewn into them or through their very material—scraps of relatives' dresses, for example. As I discuss further in chapter 4, many women writing from, about, or through borders deliberately hearken back to the homespun, to women's traditional talent for bridging home and community, private and public spheres, the artistic and the functional.

A Chicana, Gloria Anzaldúa identifies with other histories as well, her Indian ancestry, for example. In one of her several creative-critical amalgams, *Borderlands/La Frontera,* she explains: "In the ethno-poetics and performance of the shaman, my people, the Indians, did not split the artistic from the functional, the sacred from the secular, art from everyday life. The religious, social, and aesthetic purposes of art were all intertwined" (66).[6] Further, Anzaldúa claims, the way in which story (prose and poetry, or even a book of Freud's writings, for example) transforms the storyteller and listener into something or someone else is shamanistic. Because she so closely identifies her writing with her life (73), the writer as well as her story can be called "shape-changer" or shaman. Her personal history as the daughter of three cultures—Indian, Spanish, Anglo—makes her "vulnerable to foreign ways of seeing." She becomes a *"nahual,* able to transform herself into a tree, a coyote, another person" (83); in African-American lore, she would be a conjure woman. In my own terms, she is an alchemist of genres.

Inevitably the works that best exemplify and justify the crossover and even cross-fire mode are those by writers who have had literal, geographic borders to cross, those writers exiled from both home and dominant, white, heterosexist, bourgeois culture. But even the writings of Anzaldúa and Cherríe Moraga, with their alchemical, shamanistic piecing together of their pasts and their presents as they write of geographic and cultural border crossings, resemble sewing or quilting sessions; both *Borderlands/La Frontera* and *Loving in the War Years* are mosaics, patchworks of genres. Moira Monteith observes that many women writers and critics are concerned "with the theory and practice of re-writing, of pulling a text out of a previous text, . . . of creating a place in language where different voices can be heard" (5). Anzaldúa and Moraga, along with Griffin, Piercy, Rich, Tess Gallagher, and Alice Walker, have a penchant for this kind of rewriting: they put older texts, perhaps poems, into newer ones, such as essays further embroidering the poems. Such intertextuality itself hearkens back to what could be called the inter-texture-ality of women's weaving and quilting. (For a discussion of intertextual interleafing in Piercy, Gallagher, Walker, and Griffin, see chapter 4.)

Mary Daly's recurrent trope of spinning ("All mother goddesses spin and weave") in *Gyn/Ecology* doesn't immediately suggest borders of any kind except that spinning is part of the weaving process; taken together, spinning and weaving suggest to me what border crossing in general does—an ongoing creative process joining together perhaps disparate elements. This process inevitably joins the old (if not materials then technique) to the new, just as feminist poet-critics join their past work and past lives with/in their present experiments and experience. Women often write in scraps or fragments of time and may scrape together a text out of fragments of memories, scraps of their material and historical origins. As Judy Grahn has said in *The Queen of Wands* (1982), a book of poems whose major character is called Spider Webster, webster being "a word that formerly meant 'female weaver,'" "Language is a form of weaving too, a clothing our ideas wear, a glowing flesh they are made out of, a heart that beats in them" (xiii). Grahn values and describes weavers and weaving as feminist and industrial, and mechanized manufacturing of materials as enslaving, dispiriting, unspiritual. In the notes to her poems, Grahn elaborates upon several of the spinsters the poems evoke. Grahn speaks of the "Spinning Damsel of China" (95), the "Spider Grandmother" considered by many Indian tribes "their oldest and most venerated deity" (98), and similar figures occurring in Mayan, African (94), and Japanese mythology (98). "Spinster," Grahn writes, "is a word that has kept its history as a name for women who do not marry, who are sexually self-determined and even lesbian" (100)—as Grahn, Griffin, Daly, Anzaldúa, Moraga, and Rich are. Considering spinsters powerful figures individually and collectively, Grahn verbally weaves together all these mythic prototypes.

I mean to carry on this quilting or weaving tradition myself as I continue to line up or elide one notion of border with others: geographic borders, for example, may be linked to those of cloth. Geographic borders, as material and historical as cloth, are often represented in cloth (flags, territorial designs) and paper. Geographic boundaries appear in women's writings of the frontier, Manifest Destiny, U.S. expansion past and present, as well as in war diaries, slave narratives, works by those colonized or exiled or otherwise transported, and more. Further, many women evoking border-crossing images were, like the great, gun-wielding women of the plains, expanding or crossing still another boundary or border, that of acceptable feminine behavior. They crossed a border simply by beginning writing. Contemporary feminists are similarly pushing (crossly, creatively) at boundaries—literal, figurative, cultural, psychological, sexual, temporal, textual.

Borders, narrow lines, can provide the form and context of composition in still other ways. I have often had to write in small pockets of time at the borders of other tasks. I have written in installments, in ribbons, in margins. Rich has graphically described her own writing in the margins, as it were: "For ten years I was reading in fierce snatches, scribbling in notebooks, writing poetry in fragments. . . . in the late fifties I was able to write, for the first time, directly about experiencing myself as a woman. The poem was jotted in fragments during children's naps, brief hours in the library, or at 3:00 a.m. after rising with a wakeful child. I despaired of doing any continuous work at this time. Yet I began to feel that my fragments and scraps had a common consciousness" (*LSS* 44). Rich couldn't write without interruptions and ultimately began to celebrate, as I do here, the pragmatic aesthetic this kind of situation requires.

Even without the pressures of childcare, I find I have a strategy, even an aesthetic, in keeping with any woman who, for whatever reasons, feels herself a borderline artist. I expend much energy over the small: the small lyric poem, the pun, the alliterative line. Like Hester Prynne, I embroider my *A*'s and days, make do with what little I have or perceive I have. Then, in an effort to make the small things into a whole, I pull texts out of previous texts, my own or others, and so lengthen my links, my woman's web of extended identity and identification. I think of the little stitches creating Emily Dickinson's fascicles, the packets of poems secretly and slyly composed. I think of Dickinson's written image of her stitches—the dashes following, and thereby extending, her short lines. Because of Hester's gift as a seamstress, the townspeople of *The Scarlet Letter* soon believed the letter that is the novel's title to stand for "Able" instead of the intended "Adultress." The move from daily ability to art—or to a sense that those fragmented daily acts in fact are art—is what recent women writers often accomplish, although not in order to valorize some notion of "high" art over "low." We mean instead to authorize our own anthologies, to celebrate an aesthetic of the many or the split making a creative collectivity, to explore an aesthetic of familiarity, invitation, emulation, relation—not of alienation, numbness, surface, coolness, as Todd Gitlin in a *New York Times Book Review* characterizes the postmodern in art and literature. Rather than some postmodern expression of perpetual alienation and decenteredness, this writing resembling a crazy quilt gestures toward the kind of women's community a quilting bee recalls, the kind of community that helped Hester learn to read herself differently.

But women's writing, especially when it ventures beyond the tidy and domestic, seems to enter the "wild zone" Showalter describes (262), an often dangerous rather than freeing designation. Too often such work is marginalized once again: if not constantly interruptible and indoors, it is viewed, negatively, as wildly unapproachable, wildly unacceptable besides. So Griffin, with her internalized patriarchal censors, feared she was "wildly in error" (*MFE* 231); Michelene Wandor feels her "wide and wild and sometimes varied" voices may not be heard (86); and Jane Tompkins, who called in 1977 for critics to read and write "not as if they were somebody else, or as if they weren't human at all, but as and for themselves, whoever they are" ("Criticism and Feeling" 178), nonetheless continues to recognize, in her 1987 article, that "to break with conventions is to risk not being heard at all" ("Me and My Shadow").

For some of my readers, in fact, the works I have chosen to discuss may be disturbing anomalies and, because relatively new and difficult to classify, unworthy of critical consideration or consideration *as* criticism. But I propose they exemplify a paradigm shift (to build on Thomas Kuhn's oft-borrowed phrase), this time in critical discourse.[7] It is no longer true that Adrienne Rich's *Of Woman Born,* which critic Maggie Humm termed "an original form of feminist criticism in its mix of anthropology, literature, and autobiography," has "not been succeeded by any criticism as ambitious or hybrid a form" (96). Following composition theory's emphasis on process, the demise of New Criticism, and the rise of reader-response theory, poet-critics are in ascendance. As partial proof, Tompkins managed to complete and publish her hybrid academic article, "Me and My Shadow," Griffin published not only the text she questioned herself about but others, and Wandor published several works as well. The proof is only partial because Tompkins might not have been able to publish her article were she not already a well-known, well-published critic; the paradigm shift is still in progress. The misgivings of and challenge to those in the borderlands—between creative and academic writers, tenure-track teachers and not, the published and the perished—continues.

The Examples of Gloria Anzaldúa, Cherrie Moraga, Maxine Hong Kingston, and Adrienne Rich

We will have different histories, but we will often have similar struggles.
>Caren Kaplan, "Deterritorializations: The Rewriting of Home and Exile in Western Feminist Discourse" (1987)

Paradoxically, the more we hear about the experiences of each particular group, the more we learn how much we share as a community of women and how often our commonalities cross cultural and racial barriers.
>Amy Ling, "I'm Here: An Asian American Woman's Response" (1988)

The recent explosions in Black American and American feminist literatures have invigorated and revived the American literary scene and challenged the institutional canon. Chicana writers, likewise, are joining and expanding the frontiers of Americas' belles lettres.
>Maria Herrera-Sobek, *Chicana Creativity and Criticism: Charting New Frontiers in American Literature* (1987)

Since [Chicana] experience has been traditionally excluded from literary representation, it is not surprising that writing that explores the Chicana-as-subject is often accompanied by formal and linguistic innovation. . . . The search is for a language that consciously opposes the dominant culture.
>Yvonne Yarbro-Bejarano, "Chicana Literature from a Chicana Feminist Perspective" (1987)

Obviously, examples abound in which contemporary writers, especially those women occupying a marginalized position in American society and its literature, employ the central trope of border crossing as both theme and compositional mode, thereby writing their composite selves into a rich textuality. Poetic prose, often an amalgam of genres, a crossing of various borders, may enable women to abandon patriarchal discourse for a discourse of unbounded fecundity. For poet-critics Anzaldúa, Moraga, Maxine Hong Kingston, and Rich, who are hybrids in their cultural and even writerly identities, problematic actual border crossings become metaphorically fertile. In *Borderlands,* Anzaldúa foregrounds border crossing as the chief mode of her life and language, and asserts she will face and overlap the borders of her many selves, countries, and cultures in her multivoiced writing: "I will no longer be made to feel ashamed of existing. I will have my voice: Indian, Spanish, White. I will have my serpent's tongue—my woman's voice, my sexual voice" (59). She tells us that her writing "transforms living in the Borderlands from a nightmare into a numinous experience. It is always a path/state to something else" (73). It is this writing that is always in process, on the verge of change, combining poetry and prose—or the spirit of poetry with varieties of interdisciplinary prose—that I call alchemical and find characteristic of more and more feminists from a range of disciplines.[8]

In Anzaldúa's *Borderlands* and Moraga's *Loving in the War Years,* the poet-critic strives to exist in a world that would criticize the poet and the woman writer as it does the lesbian and Chicana. As lesbians, according to Anzaldúa, they are with male homosexuals "the supreme crossers of cultures" (84) and reside in a kind of war zone or "shock culture" (11). Anzaldúa's and Moraga's multiple identities have long been as problematical as (their) lives lived literally in the borderlands, on the Texas-Mexico or California-Mexico border. They rely more heavily on border imagery than Kingston or Rich: it is still possible for their crossing from homeland to homeland, language to language, to occur daily, by choice if not necessity. Chinese-American Maxine Hong Kingston, though not crossing from prose to poetry or from one language to another as do Anzaldúa and Moraga, addresses in part the problem of the poet along with that of Chinese-American woman writer. Her mixed-genre books, *Woman Warrior* and *China Men,* cross other kinds of generic borders, swerve between autobiography and fiction, myth and reality, sometimes expressed in the form of historical statistics. Rich, a lesbian and child of an interfaith couple, tries in "Split at the Root: An Essay on Jewish Identity" and the poem "Sources," among other writings, to heal her split identity(ies). For these four authors, borders and hybridization are decidedly more than a metaphor or a making of mixed genres.

Borders both join and separate (just as sewing brings together everyday materials in a domestic economy coupling art with survival, in a system underscoring the separation of the sewing circle from masculine quarters). Borders suggest limitations, that which is prohibited and forbidden and in a constant state of transition (or what Anzaldúa calls "psychic unrest"). It can be risky to try to migrate across a border, whether aesthetic or geographic. As I observe above, in crossing or defying literary genres or conventions one risks not being heard. More disturbingly, in attempting to cross the Mexican-U.S. border, for example, too many would-be immigrants are suffocated in boxcars, lost in the desert, or drowned in the Rio Grande. Migrating boat people drown. Simply contemplating one's hybrid history can be unsettling and painful. Writing it all down can alienate a writer from the very roots and relatives she attempts to remember and write toward. Further, it can get her fired or never hired, blacklisted, excommunicated, or exiled.

This alienation I speak of, or Anzaldúa, Moraga, and Kingston speak of, is similar to but more immediate and less abstract than the Lacanian notion that one becomes a "subject," gains selfhood, only by losing one's previous sense of oneness with the mother. When one comes into language and is thus able to name the (absent) mother, mother is then doubly distanced from oneself, the subject: she is invoked and yet erased by language. Language is elegy to the thing; it both evokes and evades. Language expresses "not-I" even as it attempts to express the "I."[9] But here I'd like to displace/efface Lacan and his followers, inheritors. The linguistic experiments and the expe-

rience of alienation and problematic multiple identities I speak
of derive not so much from a postmodern plight or poststructur-
alist perspective as from the centuries-old phenomena of rac-
ism, sexism, heterosexism, ethnocentrism, ablism, and other
forms of discrimination.

Danger has long lurked in the borderlands. It's risky to
succeed in border crossing, in the making of a new life, in
assimilating. Inside, one is perhaps even more the outsider, the
migrant, the marginal. According to Anzaldúa, "Gringos in the
U.S. Southwest consider the inhabitants of the borderlands
transgressors, aliens—whether they possess documents or not,
whether they're Chicanos, Indians or Blacks. Do not enter,
trespassers will be raped, maimed, strangled, gassed, shot. . . .
Ambivalence and unrest reside there and death is no stranger"
(3–4). If one survives, one may nonetheless become alienated
from one's former self, relatives, and friends. The mother of
Kingston's relative "Mad Sao" felt abandoned in China; de-
picted as a liar and nagger, however, she seemed responsible for
Sao's madness derived from his guilt. Other men who had left
China for America took new, American wives and abandoned
their first wives in China. Even Kingston's own mother, "Brave
Orchid," was told by her husband, who spoke the law of the
white fathers, that she couldn't come to America without a
Western education: "Get a degree. Send it to me as evidence you
are educated, and I'll send you a ship ticket" (*China Men* 65). In
many ways, then, the women suffered more than the men who
had had to stow away in crates on ships (49) or toil dangerously
to build a mountain railroad (121–49).

Few crossings are without cost, and most are motivated by
an already bad situation or a prior sense of being torn. Rich feels
the "history of denial within [her] like an injury" (*BBP* 122). Her
father's denying that his Jewishness mattered and her own
long denial of half her heritage hurt. Moraga explains that her
book is one her family will never see: "It is difficult to separate
in my mind whether it is my writing or my lesbianism which
has made me an outsider to my family" (iv). Her work both
records and perpetuates a separation at the same time as it
demonstrates sometimes problematic connections (here, for ex-

ample, Moraga finds it "difficult to separate" her writing and her lesbianism).

On the other hand, borders also suggest positive associations for these writers. While ocean and shore may often overlap in a "violent clash," at other times they experience a "gentle coming together," Anzaldúa observes in her opening poem (1). She speaks optimistically about Mexican philosopher Jose Vascocelos's theory of inclusivity, of races coming together and creating an enriched gene pool: "At the confluence of two or more genetic streams, with chromosomes constantly 'crossing over,' this mixture . . . rather than resulting in an inferior being, provides a hybrid progeny, a mutable, more malleable species with a rich gene pool" (77). Anzaldúa's prose, itself a malleable hybrid, shifts to a poem asserting, "I, a mestiza, / continually walk out of one culture / and into another / . . . I am in all cultures at the same time (77). Just as her book oscillates between prose and poetry, Anzaldúa's words operate on the border between literal and metaphoric meaning. Borders and crossings-over are thus both her message and her means of expression. For Moraga, writing functions not only to separate herself from her family (because she cannot share her work with them); it frees her to "love them from places in [herself] that had before been mired in unexpressed pain. Writing has ultimately brought [her] back to them" (v).

Anzaldúa confides, "Being a writer feels very much like being a Chicana, or being queer—a lot of squirming, coming up against all sorts of walls. Or its opposite: nothing defined or definite, a boundless, floating state of limbo" (72). For Anzaldúa, writing is a space she resists and yet one which, finally entered, takes her back to herself. Ultimately, all these border-zone works attempt to make more definite, or at the least, depict, their authors' lives in the borderlands or wild zone. They carry their authors across the border from present to past. They reach out to roots and readers.

Anzaldúa's title foregrounds her history on the border between the U.S. and Mexico and accounts for (and replicates) her book's frequent crossings from English to Spanish,[10] prose to poetry, autobiography to history. Cherrie Moraga's title also evokes an image of a border zone between the neighboring countries of love and destruction. She, like Anzaldúa, identifies with Chicana/Indian/lesbian cultures. Born in California and raised in New York City, Moraga perceives that being a Chicana lesbian in a racist, homophobic, misogynist country means loving as if in a militarized zone, in war years. In the metadiscourse common to feminist writing, Moraga makes clear the generic, topical, and linguistic border crossings such a simultaneously loving and embattled writer must make:

> Some days I feel my writing wants to break itself open. Speak in a language that maybe no "readership" can follow. What does it mean that the Chicana writer if she truly follows her own voice, she may depict a world so specific, so privately ours, so full of "foreign" language to the anglo reader, there will be no publisher. . . . I have been translating my experience out of fear of an aloneness too great to bear. I have learned analysis as a mode to communicate what I feel the experience itself already speaks for. The combining of poetry and essays in this book is the compromise I make in the effort to be understood. In Spanish, "compromiso" is also used to mean obligation or commitment. And I guess, in fact, I write as I do because I *am committed* to communicating with both sides of myself . . . Chicana and anglo. (vi)

To Moraga, border-crossing writing is both a compromise (an unwanted or burdensome "translation") and a choice, a commitment. Moraga's essays (where most of the "analysis" occurs) are a concession to an imagined readership requiring and admiring critical discourse. Poetry, that analog to or embodier of "the experience itself," is not enough. Poems comprise about one-fifth of her book; the rest can be described as memoirs, journal entries, criticism, and diatribes.

For her part, Anzaldúa calls for a "massive uprooting of dualistic thinking" in order to heal the splits she and others have experienced at the root of "our" culture, language, and thought (80). She then labels herself cultureless because, as a feminist, she challenges collective cultural, religious, male-derived beliefs of Indo-Hispanics and Anglos; but she is cultured because

she is participating in the creation of yet another culture (81).
She insists that despite internal and external contradictions—
certainly the plight of Moraga as well—she will "survive the
crossroads." She is "both/either," straddling and striving be-
yond borders, the limits of language, genre, state, nation, cul-
ture. She refuses either to deny or to limit her identity, and her
refusal is enacted, like Moraga's, in her moving from prose to
poetry, from one language, one genre, to another.

Anzaldúa's opening poem, "El otro México," which follows,
contains the informing metaphors for her life and text:

Wind tugging at my sleeve
feet sinking into the sand
I stand at the edge where earth touches ocean
where the two overlap
a gentle coming together
at other times and places a violent clash.

Across the border in Mexico
  stark silhouette of houses gutted by waves,
    cliffs crumbling into the sea
      silver waves marbled with spume

        gashing a hole under the border fence.
            Miro el mar atacar
            la cerca en Border Field Park
          con sus buchones de agua
        an Easter Sunday resurrection
        of the brown blood in my veins.
Oigo el llorido del mar, el respiro del aire,
  my heart surges to the beat of the sea.
    In the gray haze of the sun
      the gulls' shrill cry of hunger
        the tangy smell of the sea seeping into me.

      I walk   through the hole in the fence
        to the other side
    Under my fingers I feel the gritty wire
        rusted by 139 years
          of the salty breath of the sea.

Beneath the iron sky
Mexican children kick their soccer ball across,
run after it, entering the U.S.
    I press my hand to the steel curtain—
    chainlink fence crowned with rolled barbed wire—
rippling from the sea where Tijuana touches San Diego
    unrolling over mountains
        and plains
            and deserts,
this "Tortilla Curtain" turning into *el rio Grande*
    flowing down to the flatlands
        of the Magic Valley of South Texas
    its mouth emptying into the Gulf.

1,950 mile-long open wound
        dividing a *pueblo,* a culture,
          running down the length of my body,
            staking fence rods in my flesh,
          splits me   splits me
           me raja   me raja
    This is my home
    this thin edge of
      barbwire.

    But the skin of the earth is seamless.
    The sea cannot be fenced.
    el mar does not stop at borders.
To show the white man what she thought of his
           arrogance,
      Yemaya blew that wire fence down.

      This land was Mexican once,
        was Indian always
        and is.
              And   will be again.

    Yo soy un puente tendido
      del mundo gabacho al del mojado,
    lo pasado me estira pa' 'tras
      y lo presente pa' 'delante.
    Que la Virgen de Guadalupe me cuide
    Ay ay ay, soy mexicana de este lado.

The line beginning "I walk" (typo)graphically illustrates the poet/speaker's movement "through the hole in the fence/to the other side." She does this walking with writing, the verbal equivalent of the (soccer) playing that enables Mexican children to enter the U.S., at least temporarily. Playfully, painfully, Anzaldúa makes her readers enter holes or splits in her lines, psyche, life, portraying her people's split and also doubled culture, her being split amongst origins and destinations in the split and doubled line, "splits me   splits me." The tenuousness and danger of this plight is underscored in the thinnest lines of the poem, where the "thin edge of / barbwire" sticks out like the material it is supposed to represent.

Anzaldúa's images alternate between the grounded and the atmospheric, the "gritty wire" of the line and the expansiveness of the mood, imagery, and stanza breaks. Like the sea, the poem's expansiveness cannot be fenced: *"el mar* does not stop at borders" (1. 51). For an English-speaking reader with no knowledge of Spanish or a Spanish speaker without English, the language of the free-verse poem and thus its author's life are mysterious, not completely translatable; their meaning is in limbo. Not even the dividing lines are clear: the lines are enjambed and the Spanish alternately goes beyond, reiterates, and is overwhelmed by the English, except in the final stanza, which is all in Spanish. Perhaps Anzaldúa's readers, particularly those used to privilege of whatever kind, need to experience borders they cannot cross or, like Anzaldúa, a "boundless, floating state of limbo"; they need to be reminded that they/I do not know, cannot have, everything. The marginal perspective is that edifying.

The final stanza, all in italicized Spanish, resembles prayerful murmuring. Italicized speech seems ghostlike, like voices from beyond, and this final passage refers to "la Virgen de Guadalupe," a goddess we learn elsewhere is "the single, most potent religious, political and cultural image of the Chicano/ *mexicano.*" La Virgen de Guadalupe is, like Anzaldúa's ethnic identity as well as her text, " a synthesis of the old world and the new, of the religion and culture of the two races in [the Chicano] psyche, the conquerors and the conquered" (30). La Virgen de Guadalupe mediates between cultures, between humans and the divine; she symbolizes the "tolerance for ambiguity" that people of mixed races, people who cross cultures, "by necessity possess" (30)—and which readers of poems must learn.

After all, poems are characteristically mediators full of or symbolizing ambiguity. Poetry creates pleasure or insight along with connections between vehicle and tenor, the sound of one word and the sound of another—thus mediating between reader and writer, literal and figurative, this world and an imagined other. And yet, so much poetry is also a finally untranslatable mix of gritty details bordered by the inchoate expansiveness of both the poet's and the reader's emotions and associations. Anzaldúa's prose clarification of *border* also might be describing poetry as it looks on the page, poetry as it is created and received: "A border is a dividing line, a narrow strip along a steep edge. A borderland is a vague and undetermined place created by the emotional residue of an unnatural boundary. It is in a constant state of transition" (3).

Like borders of countries and the geographical features—such as rivers—that define them, poetry is in a "constant state of transition." Lines of poetry, like borders, represent both division and connection, clarity and vagueness/vagaries at once. Poet-autobiographer Patricia Hampl reminds us that the value of the ancient science of alchemy is like that of poetry, and both of these are like anthologistic, changeling, cross-genre works. "The golden light of metaphor, which is the intelligence of poetry, was implicit in alchemical study. To change, magically, one substance into another, more valuable one is the ancient function of metaphor, as it was of alchemy" (Hampl 219). Mary Daly urges women to use the ways they have been circumscribed or closed out as raw material for a process of alchemy. In *Gyn/Ecology,* she suggests women "transmute the base metals of man-made myth by becoming unmute, calling forth from ourselves and each other the courage to name the unnameable" (34). Poets are especially suited to this transformative task. Anzaldúa even explicitly likens her people—which is to say, herself and her writing, given how they intertwine in her mind—to a "great alchemical work; spiritual *mestizaje,* a 'morphogenesis'" (81).

"The gold of the alchemists was," Hampl insists, not evidence of the "common avarice of the kings and princes who were greedy and credulous enough to employ magicians for outlandish purposes," but spiritual and transformative, the token of exchange and the substance of *change* (219). Poetry both prepares one for and expresses a life of change, of both aiding and evading conventions. Anzaldúa is as much a "protean being" as the poem she begins with these two words (41). "Poetry is no respecter of convention" agrees Griffin ("Poetry as a Way of Knowledge," *MFE* 246). Piercy, who says she writes in organic verse, "the predominant poetic form of our time" (*PCB* 29), observes that "poetry is a type of knowing which is only partly rational" (24): "the observers *change* what they observe" (27; emphasis mine). And for those feminists writing personally but not necessarily poetically or in actual poetry, I still like to think the term *poet-critic* applies: the poet part of their writerly identity comes from their being visionaries, their insistence on making connections and changes, their foregrounding the dangers and delights of language. As a poet and a critic, I am attracted to their anomalous, mixed-genre writing because it frees me similarly to meld literary and life studies, poetry and prose, to advocate changes of word and world. Border-crossing writing draws me to the threshold of myself, woos me too to write. Interactive, fluid discourse invites readers to change or "alchemize" themselves into writers, to cross borders both textual and psychological.

Much of the border-crossing power behind Maxine Hong Kingston's work is characterized by Sui Sin Far's sentiment in "Leaves from the Mental Portfolio of a Eurasian," "So I roam backward and forward across the continent. When I am East, my heart is West. When I am West, my heart is East. Before long I hope to be in China. As my life began in my father's country it may end in my mother's" (189). In *The Woman Warrior* (1976) and *China Men* (1980), Kingston rejects Chinese and western culture only to turn around again and embrace them. *The Woman Warrior* and *China Men* do not make the self-disclosing statements (those direct statements about both the author and her compositional strategies) prevalent in Anzaldúa's and Moraga's texts, but Kingston's works similarly move from cultural history to autobiography and from criticism to nostalgia in their portrayal of the author's Chinese ancestors and their adaptation to America. Kingston's work—novelistic, historical, and partly autobiographical as it is—can also be read as feminist criticism, as, certainly, Anzaldúa's and Moraga's books can be. That is to say, all these women's works exist in borderlands overlapping the conventional realms of fiction, poetry, criticism, confession, autobiography, reportage, cultural anthropology, and history. Each author-narrator finds herself stretched, as if she were a world divided, yet each is enriched by the amalgam her anomalous writing creates and reflects.

The Woman Warrior begins by devoting itself to the problematic histories of Kingston's grandmother, mother, and aunt, while *China Men* describes in detail the history and ancestry of Kingston's father and brother. As Jean Barker-Nunn suggests, Kingston's work questions, even blurs, the conventional boundaries "between past and present, public and private, history and myth, old world and new world, family and self" (56). Barker-Nunn attributes Kingston's border crossing to the fact that "girls, unlike boys, tend to define themselves in connection to rather than separation from the mother, and thus have more difficulty drawing ego boundaries between other and self" (60).[11] Taken individually and together, Kingston's two books also thus question and cross gender roles. The woman warrior section of the first book, about which much recent criticism has been written, in part shows woman as man—woman in a conventional manly role, that of warrior, which is in turn linked to the role of the writer or those persons, usually men, whom society empowers to speak.[12]

Kingston's gender theory is revealed in the fablelike first chapter of *China Men,* "On Discovery." In it, a Chinese man named Tang Ao, "looking for the Gold Mountain, crossed an ocean, and came upon the Land of Women." In order to find the mythical Gold Mountain (China's nineteenth-century image of the riches of the United States), one must "cross an ocean"—a border separating China from America, the land of men from the "Land of Women," men from women. In this story, the man becomes a woman by being treated as one, which is also how females become women, after all. He is equipped with "pots of makeup, mirrors, and a woman's clothes" (1). His ears are pierced and his feet are cracked and bound. He adopts female accessories, female postures, and "women's food," eschewing all masculine roles—that of scholar, for example. The women sing footbinding songs: "Use aloe for binding feet and not for scholars" (2). The man's eyebrows are plucked and his feet strapped to curved shoes; his hips (now necessarily) sway and his shoulders swivel.

Reading this, the men in classes I teach grow angry, somehow believing that this has really happened to one of their kind. Without sympathy for Kingston's female kin or mine, they cry out their moral indignation: "Two wrongs don't make a right!" I try to point out that because men hold the power in Kingston's two cultures, her portrait of a single disenfranchised man doesn't pose the same danger a male's portrayal of a subdued and subordinated woman might. Lynn Sukenick puts it well: "For male writers . . . wrestling matches with silence come out of a tradition of verbal strength . . . [but] for women writers, silence has greater relevance and danger, for it is all too congruent with their alleged destiny" (44). I go on to say to my students that the event in *China Men* is only verbal and that such verbal power is ironic: women rarely shape, control, and enslave men as men do women even in modern societies. In fact, women also have long been denied both linguistic and artistic power, forbidden either to speak or to write; that is to say, across a wide range of cultures and classes, women have been bound and gagged, if not literally, then literarily. Later in Kingston's novel, they see that only China's men could learn poetry, take the Imperial Examination, become teachers or something better—that men had power to shape both themselves and "their" women. My students eventually find it interesting that they are so willing to blur fiction with fact, a mythological man's life with their own. From Kingston, these female and male readers gain all kinds of transformative, alchemical powers, the way the women who told Kingston the stories she records and embellishes gave her the power Anzaldúa would call shamanistic or characteristic of a *nahual*.

What changes for my students is what changes for Kingston later in the text. The implied misanthropy is clearly also sympathy; the two emotions, like Kingston's two cultures, are entwined. Chinese men could no longer aspire to become poets; the Imperial Examinations were suspended. In America, Chinese men worked long hours at dangerous tasks—in the dust of the Sandalwood Mountains, in the jarring and exploded rock of the Sierra Nevadas. They were subjected to the Chinese-exclusion laws, special taxes, deportations, and immigration quotas detailed in the documentary-style chapter "The Laws." Our hearts go out to them along with those even more frequent victims, women of nondominant races and cultures. Kingston and her readers appreciate as well as repudiate her parents in this text, which constitutes Kingston's (new) in-process, hybrid self.

The autobiographical-historical-fictive amalgam that is *China Men* primarily documents the lives of Chinese men—the narrator's relatives and others like them—people blessed by opportunity and distressed by discrimination, danger, change. But the lives of men depend on those of women, and Kingston's women are nearly as complex an amalgam as her writing is. They are strong, capable like Brave Orchid of obtaining a Chinese medical degree, but they also perpetuate Chinese and American patriarchy's denigration of women and exaltation of men. They submitted to footbinding and silencing. Kingston tells us of a black grandmother who "jabbered like a monkey" when she came to China only to fall mute when no one answered her (83). Kingston's own grandmother calls a baby girl ugly, angry that her husband tried to trade their son for one: "trading a son for a slave. Idiot" (16). Thus the grandmother is implicated in patriarchy as she reinscribes the patriarchal perspective of women and girls as useless apart from their potential for exploitation.

If he succeeded in making the trade, the grandfather promised, he would treat his new daughter with more love and care than that typically accorded daughters in traditional Chinese culture. Kingston intimates that where change is possible, much that is new and positive might be learned. She seems to grieve that poetry, whose magic is changing one thing into another, joining things, healing splits, is no longer a force either in Chinese or American society. In "The Li Sao: An Elegy," Kingston speaks of China's earliest known poet, Ch'u Yuan, a minister who advised peace, not war. His was an unpopular opinion, and he was exiled as an enemy of the state. After many tribulations, he drowned himself in despair at the lack of wisdom in the world. Afterward, "the people realized his sincerity and their loss" and tried to call him back (259). Only the promise of women singing new songs, the chanting of poems, and the preparing of special food could lure him back. In this way, women artists make possible both the healing and the cultural rereading/revising that border-crossing writing urges and emblemizes.

Critic King-Kok Cheung's view of *The Woman Warrior* (and Alice Walker's *Color Purple*) could apply to all these texts: "As they venture beyond linguistic norms, they perpetuate and revitalize the polyglot strains peculiar to America" (172). Readers and writers of cross-genre and polyglot works all must learn something like what Anzaldúa recognizes as necessary for the *mestiza,* for whom "rigidity means death": "The new *mestiza* copes by developing a tolerance for contradictions, a tolerance for ambiguity. . . . She learns to juggle cultures. She has a plural personality, she operates in a pluralistic mode. . . . she turns the ambivalence into something else" (79). These writers find a kind of peace in the piecework of cross-genre or multilingual passages. "The 'alien' element has become familiar—never comfortable, not with society's clamor to uphold the old, to rejoin the flock, to go with the herd. No, not comfortable, but home," Anzaldúa asserts in her preface.

Because Kingston speaks of the literal binding of women's feet under patriarchy, its stripping women of mobility (women cannot walk on tiny feet but only totter, helped along by a man or a wall), while she also demonstrates the self-awareness now possible for a woman like herself, her words and work particularize or embody Julia Penelope (Stanley) and Susan J.

Wolfe's description of a feminine aesthetic. In "Consciousness as Style; Style as Aesthetic," Penelope and Wolfe propose that a feminist aesthetic "encompasses the cultural and social attempts to cripple women, to bind us, to strip us of our self-awareness, and it also traces the unwinding of the patriarchal bonds that have limited our perceptions and descriptions of our experience" (136). In feminist art, they argue, "walls fall away; what had been perceived as boundaries melt; categories become shape-changers; sentences are never complete because the perceiving is the movement itself" (137). While Penelope and Wolfe might fail to address the importance of racial and class differences, and they posit a figurative image of crippled women without recognizing its reverberation with some Chinese women's literal fates, their language here nonetheless resonates with the shape-changing, boundary-blurring textual aesthetics of Anzaldúa, Moraga, Kingston, and Rich.

In closing without closure, Adrienne Rich's "Split at the Root: An Essay in Jewish Identity" (*BBP*) demonstrates the ongoingness of the feminist sentence and sentience. Rich maintains, "This essay, then, has no conclusions: it is another beginning for me. . . . It's a moving into accountability, enlarging the range of accountability. I know that in the rest of my life, the next half century or so, every aspect of my identity will have to be engaged" (123). Rich's process of articulating her progress through not only her ideas but also the essay form itself demonstrates her commitment to the "accountability" about which she speaks. At the outset of the essay, Rich situates herself in the present tense, where she is stuck staring at her typewriter keyboard, full of fear and shame. She shares with Anzaldúa and Moraga their border-crossing, self-disclosing metadiscursiveness, though the shape of Rich's piece is not the border-crossed mosaic of their work and Kingston's. Rich's prose doesn't erupt into extended verse or even the fabulous fairy tales of *China Men* and *The Woman Warrior*. But like Anzaldúa, Moraga, and Kingston, Rich centrally employs the notion of a split/separation/division/border while nonetheless tying herself and her dilemma to others similarly in "a state of psychic unrest."

Like them, Rich must overcome a tradition of silence. She asserts, in a performative utterance—which enacts what it announces—that she has to break her father's "silence, his taboos; in order to claim him [she has] in a sense to expose him" (101). Arnold Rich's silence seems simultaneously idiosyncratic, a product of the dominant U.S. culture wherein males do not speak of their feelings and past, as well as an example of Jewish self-denial. That is, some Jews, even when (relatively) free from threats of death and discrimination, feel that without their Jewishness all would go right with their world. They deny their past and present pain, their past and present identity. Silenced by her parents also, Kingston recalls how she was explicitly forbidden ever to speak of her aunt, her father's sister (No Name Woman of *The Woman Warrior*). Not only was the unnamed aunt thus negated, however; Kingston-as-interlocuter-and-narrator was negated or silenced too. The culture of Kingston's parents forbids anyone to speak of a shamed woman; she is disowned, treated as if never born. Such a silencing is an extreme version of the injunction to silence seemingly practiced throughout the culture—children are not to ask too many questions, and so on. Yet ultimately, in the record or reminiscence that is her book, Kingston overcomes her silence, exposing her parents' prohibitions while bringing forth an imaginative, plausible story for her lost aunt and claiming a positive identity for herself as well.

Rich vows to break her father's taboos, his conventions, and does so, in part, by beginning and ending her essay unconventionally, self-disclosingly. Only by writing out (and out of) her pain can she begin to stop feeling "Split at the root, neither Gentile nor Jew, / Yankee nor rebel" (101). So she speaks of her father's and her own early erasures or denials in prose that begins journalistically, moves to the brief quotation above from an early poem ("Readings of History"), reviews her own education as an unaffiliated then affiliated Jew, and ends with a statement of work-still-in-progress, no final borderlines drawn.

Rich confides that throughout her experiences as Portia in *The Merchant of Venice* (carefully coached in Jew-baiting by her father), her viewing of Allied-liberation newsreels of concentration camps, her friendships with Jewish women in college, and her marriage to a Jewish man with whom she raised three Jewish sons, she suffered the ambivalence that is echoed even at/in the end of her essay. Moreover, just as in her life she found herself drifting into closer association with Jews and Judaism with a less than full, perhaps faulty, understanding of why, Rich moves associatively in her essay from description to description, experiencing still, she admits, "lapses in meaning, those blanks . . . ignorance" (123).

She's not entirely clear about what all her rumination and remembrance come to, but I suppose I feel I cannot similarly allow "lapses in meaning" or avoid concluding—even though I celebrate fluid rather than definite borders. "Split at the Root" reminds writers and readers of our need to trace continually our (many) lines flowing to the past and toward the future. We learn that though able to see only from "disconnected angles" (in Rich's case, "white, Jewish, anti-Semite, racist, anti-racist, once-married, lesbian, middle-class, feminist, exmatriate southerner, *split at the root*"), we might manage regardless to find peace and inspiration in the patchwork by putting all we can on a page.

"Sources" (1982), a long poem written the same year as—and twice repeating the first phrase of—"Split at the Root: An Essay in Jewish Identity," similarly explores the question of Rich's right to affiliate with Jews, her right to a Jewish spiritual heritage. "Sources" begins with an image not fully articulated: "Old things, diffuse, unnamed, lie strong across my heart" (*Sources* 10). Rich explains that "somehow, somewhere / every poem of mine must repeat those questions": "*With whom do you believe your lot is cast? / From where does your strength come?* (*Sources* 12). In "Readings of History," "Split at the Root," and "Sources," among other works, Rich goes back again and again to questions of her roots, with her relations to her Jewishness, her dead father, and her ex-husband still unresolved, still in progress. By casting her lot/recognizing her lot with the wandering Jew, Rich also becomes the ever-wondering Jew. "Wearing the Star of David / on a thin chain at [her] breastbone" (*Sources* 24), Rich makes clear that she has chosen to identify as a Jew; even so, her links, like the chain, may continue to be "thin," tenuous. Among her other uncertainties, she wonders how can she identify with the religion of her father(s) and husband when they represent "the face of patriarchy," "the kingdom of the fathers" (15). She then states more firmly, "The Jews I've felt rooted among / are those who were turned to smoke" (*Sources* 24). Yet the phrase "turned to smoke," a phrase simultaneously devastatingly historical-literal and casually vernacular-figurative, ambiguously suggests both that Rich's Jewishness goes back past her father and that her roots have evaporated, gone up like smoke.

Rich's voice is sad, sober, determined, flip, and ironic all at once. She feels guilty for having been raised by an assimilated Jew, in or near the bigoted southern U.S., for not only "growing up safe, American" all during World War II (as a "*Southern Jew . . . split at the root, raised in a castle of air*"), but for having "had no idea of what [she] had been spared" given the "immense silence / of the Holocaust" (13). She vows to find in herself something "more than [Jewish] self-hatred," as it seems to have been practiced by her father, to find "something more than food, / humor, a turn of phrase, a gesture of the hands." Rich's struggle to convince herself comes through in her determined repetition of the words, "there is something more" (25). She closes by admitting "there is no finite knowing"; there are no clear names (as there are for the beautiful and common weeds she both read about and sees in her journeys back to New England, the ostensible inaugural source of this poem). Despite this, she writes (in the prose-poem style that characterizes three-and-a-half parts of this twelve-part poem, as if part of her were one thing and part another, as is the case) that she has made a "powerful and womanly series of choices," that she can now begin "knowing the world, and [her] place in it" (35). "Sources" thus ends less ambiguously than "Split at the Root"; it lacks a specific plan, but it does end with the hope or suggestion that through time and the force of will she will find and make her connection.

In the meantime, like Anzaldúa, Rich must tolerate, even

celebrate, contradictions, ambiguity, plurality, and change. "This is the sacrifice that the act of creation requires, a blood sacrifice. . . . And for images, words, stories to have this transformative power, they must arise from the human body—flesh and bone—and from the Earth's body—stone, sky, liquid, soil" (Anzaldúa, *Borderlands* 75). In front of the *mestiza* lies a crossroads—and a choice—according to Anzaldúa. She can choose "to feel a victim where someone else is in control and therefore responsible and to blame . . . , or to feel strong, and, for the most part, in control" (21). Anzaldúa, Moraga, Kingston, and Rich inevitably head toward strength and connection and away from victimization and dissipation. This strength comes not from rigidity, but from malleability, poetic sensitivity, a tolerance for contradictions and ambiguity, for living in border zones, in cross fire. They are like the *mestiza* who does not only "sustain the contradictions, [but] turns the ambivalence into something else" (79): a multivalenced, multigeneric text.

"Coming to terms with one's history offers a significant mode of connection and an undeniable source of power" (60), writes Barker-Nunn. If one's "terms" take tours and turns across the borders of geography, history, culture, language, ego, *and* genres and disciplines, the connection with shape-changing, poetic powers can be very great indeed. And yet, I do not want to practice what Caren Kaplan calls a "form of theoretical tourism on the part of the first world critic, where the margin becomes a linguistic or critical vacation, a new poetics of the exotic" (191). Although I link together these women writers, all of whom occupy marginalized positions in American society, and I further link myself with these border crossers in terms of both my personal history and my aesthetic practice, I do not mean to flatten out the differences among them as I propose a general theory of border-bred prose.

I have tried hard to keep the differences among and within women as prominent in my mind and text as the coalition and commonalities I often sense—and try to create—among different writers. Maria C. Lugones and Elizabeth V. Spelman suggest that being invited "to speak about being 'women' . . . in distinction from speaking about being Hispana, Black, Jewish, working-class, etc." is an invitation to silence (574). I hope that when I reinvoke a woman's need and right to her own speech I am not in any way offering an invitation to silence. I have faith that what Houston Baker called the "autobiographical negotiation of meta-levels"—or the crossing and coupling of the autobiographical with the theoretical and speculative other—can disrupt or preempt the falsely panoramic or touristic ("Theory and Poetics of African-American Women's Writing"). Because I continually negotiate or move between the specific and the general, borders of group and individual identities may blur, but I hope they are not erased. And I hope our understanding of group- and self-construction of and by texts is thereby enriched.

THREE

Con-text/uality:

Analogs,

Precedents,

Parallels to

(and More

Examples of)

Cross-Genre

Writing by

American

Feminist

Poet-Critics

*As a "contemporary" or truly post-romantic individual, "I"
exist only insofar as I write, and in so doing, write in the
place of the other. . . . This is why, for Roland Barthes—as
well as for other "contemporary" critics—criticism is ul-
timately indissociable from autobiography and from reflec-
tion on autobiography.*

> Louis A. Renza, "The Veto of the
> Imagination: A Theory of Autobiography"
> (1977)

*Criticism has always found its place within the creative act
of autobiography and now writers on autobiography have
reversed that proposition to bring the creative act of auto-
biography, clandestinely perhaps, into their criticism.*

> James Olney, *Autobiography: Essays
> Theoretical and Critical* (1980)

*Women's writing in fiction and as a theory also shares some
characteristics with postmodernism as an avant-garde
movement, including its defiance of the authoritarian past
and its extensions of language to aspects of human experi-
ence previously unexplored or unexpressed (women's expe-
rience, in the case of women's writing).*

> Martha Noel Evans, *Masks of Tradition*
> (1987)

*[James Britton] privileges private expression over public
transaction, process over product. In arguing that writing
for the self is the matrix out of which all forms of writing
develop, he valorizes an activity and a mode of expression
that have previously been undervalued or invisible, much
as feminist literary critics have argued that women's let-
ters and diaries are legitimate forms and should be studied
and taught alongside traditional genres. . . . Feminist In-
quiry and composition studies have much in common.*

> Elizabeth Flynn, "Composing as a Woman
> (1988)

Broadly speaking, all literature is cross-generic: the Bible is epi-deictic, textbook, history, parable; the epic, narrative and po-etry; the novel, as Henry James thought it, "a large baggy mon-ster," a grab bag of narrative, (social, religious) history, myth, autobiography, letters, philosophy—from *Tristram Shandy, Clarissa,* and *Daniel Deronda,* through *Ulysses, Song of Sol-omon,* and *The Handmaid's Tale.* Yet we still know what to call these works while we are less sure what to call and how to read the mixed-genre prose of a variety of contemporary feminists. Marginalized women's border-crossing critical amalgams usu-ally depend both more heavily and more obviously than novels on the autobiographical, often making explicit their practical or political as well as literary etiologies and aims. Feminist poet-critics strive to weave the practical and material aspects of their lives into a literary mosaic. Their multilayered, multivalenced textuality occasions a blend of what Jane Gallop calls two kinds of readings, the literary and the nonliterary, with the literary implying "painstaking regard for a plurality of significations" and the nonliterary demanding "reduction to a manipulable sense in the service of efficient use" (22). This blending or border crossing further occasions a readerly conflict in me: is my enthu-siasm over formal experiments like Anzaldúa's a privileging of the aesthetic over the real-world conflicts her form is designed to re-present?

Like Gallop, I worry that reading Freud or Anzaldúa as a literary text might "function as a gesture to aestheticize an ever larger realm, implying that Freud [or Anzaldúa] too is only a tissue of signifiers, not a practical attempt to understand and affect people and the world" (31). Further, it is not Freud who wrote about being in a war zone, but Anzaldúa, Moraga, Rich, and Kingston—and Gallop herself—who confess to being torn and energized at once by the exigencies and urgencies of their existence in a patriarchal, hierarchical society that divides mind from body, public from private spheres. It is their feminist metadiscourse that finally authorized me to join them in speak-ing to and out of the intertwinings of the autobiographical, criti-cal, theoretical, political, and aesthetic. Their compositional comments, explicitly conflating the personal and political, mark the difference between their cross-genre writing and that of canonical or hegemonic or otherwise less marginal transgeneric authors.

On the other hand, Wendy Lesser has argued in "Autobiography and the 'I' of the Beholder" that perhaps all Americans writing in English feel the dichotomy Chicano Richard Rodriquez has written of in his autobiography, *Hunger of Memory*. Rodriguez felt that at school, in English, he addressed "a general audience of listeners," while at home, in Spanish, he spoke privately, intimately (quoted in Lesser 28). Lesser proposes that while not all Americans grew up in bilingual homes like Rodriguez's, few of us are many generations away from that "other" language akin to Rodriguez's Spanish. We who write in American English may always feel ourselves addressing a "general audience" rather than our intimates. As Lesser theorizes, "Culture, if not strictly language, firmly divides American private life (of family, of familiarity) from the mixed, multitudinous public life, where no one can be sure how the other guy was brought up. We do not know one another automatically, as the English seem to, so when we speak to unknown audiences—as we always do when we write—we essentially speak to strangers. Or if not to strangers, then to ourselves—the sermon or the diary, the impersonal public pronouncement or the private, unshaped, whispered confession" (28). Lacanians similarly argue that we are separated from the mother/other, and from ourselves, when we (begin to) speak or write. Yet, while all of us, then, may be variously divided, writers who are women and/or of mixed or nondominant racial or ethnic heritages (many of whom live torn between motherland and the other, cultures and classes, tradition and innovation, long denied a voice in dominant or other discourse) often feel and fight—or highlight—division most intensely.

As Caren Kaplan reminds us, it makes a difference whether "deterritorialization [one term for the displacement of identities, persons, and meanings endemic to the postmodern world system] has chosen me or whether I choose it" (191). That is, who is in charge of the oscillation between margin and center, home and exile, that all these writers, and perhaps all writers, experience? In the U.S., the greater the number of the following attributes one has, the greater the chance linguistic or critical choice can be and has been exercised: white, male, heterosexual, monied, Protestant, native speaker of English, able-bodied. Rodriguez, because male, may be less displaced in American society and American English than his lesbian Chicana sisters Anzaldúa and Moraga. Perhaps the more marginalized one feels, the more one wants to blur the division between public and private life and language and to resist both dualism and separatism by crossing from language to language, genre to genre, discipline to discipline, writer to reader.

Because I am a woman writer of mixed religious and class identity, mixed up about faith, I believe marginalization has both chosen me and been chosen by me as something I wish to foreground in my life, criticism, and poetry. Like Anzaldúa, Moraga, Rich, and Kingston, I simultaneously resist being assimilated into dominant discourse and reach toward collaboration and community among genres, languages, readers, ethnic and racial minorities, American women writers, and my many selves. I also reach toward a collaboration and community of critical voices, especially in this chapter. Nonetheless, it is still obvious to me that the personal urgency and risks taken in experimental discourse are always greater for those of the non-dominant gender, race(s), ethnicities, classes, sexuality, or religion(s) writing against hierarchy and between borders than they are for most male American or European theorists well situated in the academy. In this chapter, therefore, I choose to acknowledge briefly rather than analyze in great detail a range of past and present theorists and poet-critics to whom in many ways contemporary feminist poet-critics are indebted or otherwise similar in their poetics and practices. So as not to appear either simplistic or exclusionary in my celebration of writing by contemporary American feminist poet-critics, I write this chapter somewhat along the lines of English feminist Maggie Humm's statement that "clearly it would be wrong to ignore the influences of . . . particular texts such as *S/Z*, and particular stances such as Geoffrey Hartman's definition of reading as a dialogic and creative act, on feminist criticism" (108).

In the first part of the chapter, which includes a discussion of the Salman Rushdie case, I crosshatch feminist and post-structuralist theories to reveal some of the overlaps and gaps in discourses often thought to reflect two incompatible views of language. As in the "two kinds of readings" Gallop describes, one view (usually attributed to an American or Anglo-American socio-historical strain of feminist criticism) frequently accepts an expressive, referential, and practical view of language while the other (usually attributed to poststructuralism or French feminism) sees everywhere at work a web of multiplicity and indeterminacy, finite meaning forever deferred.[1] However, the seemingly incompatible strains of feminism and poststructuralism/postmodernism nonetheless overlap in their practice of cultural criticism, their distaste for the hierarchies that inevitably result from binary oppositions in Western culture, their writing across the disciplines, and their deconstructing of conventional authority. Jonathan Holden's description of the "main task of the postmodern poet," for example, could easily be considered that of feminist poet-critics as well: a "lifelong, continuous quest for a valid style—for integrity in the face of that 'violence without'" (118).

The programs of poststructuralist and feminist critics (though not nearly so monolithic as "programs" suggests) are more or less reconcilable, after all. As the Rushdie case suggests, they both speak their resistance to authority through language and yet see that we are "spoken by" discourse(s) in ways we cannot control. The "Rushdie affair" sheds light, I think, on the intersection of (feminist) liberationist claims about language and the poststructuralist notion that the author is dead; it also sheds light on the question of whether faith equals/results in creative freedom or is incompatible with it, and whether creative freedom is in any case illusory.

As the second part of this chapter suggests, many disparate voices collectively speaking for writerly risk taking and disciplinary and generic border crossing are currently and certainly audible. American feminist poet-critics such as Jane Gallop, Catherine Stimpson, Audre Lorde, Nancy Mairs, and Louise Bernikow, highlighted in this chapter, thus both inspire and are indebted to a community of analogs, from nineteenth-century women writing in nontraditional, noncanonical modes, to writers of slave narratives, Transcendentalist writers of journals and poems, feminist consciousness-raising groups, modernist poets, and poststructuralist/postmodernist, composition, psychoanalytic, and reader-response theorists.

Reading Rushdie

Some time ago, I watched the *Phil Donahue Show* on which members of PEN spoke out about the death sentence Iran's Ayatollah Khomeini had pronounced upon Rushdie, Indianborn author of the novel *The Satanic Verses*.[2] As most of us recall, Rushdie has been condemned for writing an innovative novel his antagonists see as a satanic *versus*—a blasphemous critique of Islamic holy works and traditions. While not a poet-critic exactly, Rushdie is a creative writer whose plight is critical. On *Donahue,* one PEN member insisted that to the American and British authors supporting Rushdie, Moslems are not the enemy; censorship and violence are. Rushdie stands for all those unnamed writers censored, tortured, or killed in scenarios not monitored or public, as Rushdie's is. Moslems and the writers they abhor are simply persons of different faiths, writers having their own religion—that of the word, of the freedom to express what they like. Neither group wants its religious rights abridged.

I felt a thrill at the thought of this writers' faith. But then it occurred to me that academic writers, myself included, often act without that faith, in bad faith. We had not immediately made Rushdie and the issue of First-Amendment rights the topic of the day in the halls of academe. And, diverse theorists of creative-critical prose notwithstanding, we have too often allowed our notions of academic formalism or academic duty to censor our moral, personal, political, and creative impulses in our writing.[3]

Only alone, at home, in a situation more like that of PEN members than of most of my academic associates,[4] can I con-

template the Rushdie case, cut out articles to show my stu-
dents, find my faith again in free—or free-fall—writing (I think
of the fantastic free-fall of Rushdie's novel's opening scene, his
main characters falling from an airplane, as I freely flow from
current events through the current of my own thoughts here in
a new-old kind of nonfiction).

Another speaker on *Phil Donahue,* the poet and novelist
Erica Jong, echoed the other participants' sympathy with Mos-
lem outrage and yet horror at the retaliation the Ayatollah had
asked (and his successor continues to ask) the devout to per-
form: death to Rushdie, his publisher, his agent, and all others
continuing to distribute the novel. Jong was angry that Rush-
die's work was being condemned without actually having been
read, as one of her works once was. But Jong also asserted that
America's publishers and the corporate conglomerates that own
most of the publishing houses have themselves been a death
threat to authors before now. They also put a price on authors'
heads, she said, when they print only what readers will buy in
droves, only what is not too controversial (or they take contro-
versial works off bookstore shelves, as the Waldenbooks chain
did in the wake of Khomeini's condemnation).

And they deserve much less sympathy than the Islamic fun-
damentalists. I have been writing about women whose mothers
and sisters have been silenced, who have themselves come to
doubt the truth, safety, and efficacy of their words, but who have
nonetheless come round to alchemize forms simultaneously ex-
pressive and creative of their multiple and conflicting identities.
I have been writing of their propensity for mixed-genre, inter-
disciplinary, personal, political prose while following that pro-
pensity myself. And yet, our American-feminist faith in writing
as self-expression, the end of repression, seems naïve in an era
when the "death of the author" has been proclaimed not only by
religious fanatics but by American and European literary crit-
ics. Although perhaps in different senses of the word, both
deaths are *literal* (variously defined as "according to the letter of
the scriptures"; "actual, obvious"; "of, relating to, expressed in,
letters"). Khomeini claimed his death threat was by the letter of
his religious law; his edict calls for a murderous act to result in

actual death. In his essay "The Death of the Author," poststruc-
turalist Roland Barthes, working through the implications of
Saussurean linguistics, theorizes the death of the author, any
author.

Barthes concludes, "It is language which speaks, not the
author. . . . Linguistically, the author is never more than the
instance writing, just as *I* is nothing other than the instance
saying *I:* language knows a 'subject,' not a 'person,' and this
subject [is] empty outside of the very enunciation which defines
it" (145). In "What Is an Author?" Michel Foucault also details
the death of the author, stating that writing "has become linked
to sacrifice, even to the sacrifice of life: it is now a voluntary
effacement . . . the writing subject cancels out the signs of his
[*sic*] particular individuality. As a result, the writer is reduced
to nothing more than the singularity of his absence; he must
assume the role of the dead man in the game of writing" (142–
43). Where there is no "central signified" (after Derrida), there
is no central signifier, either.

I am intrigued by several questions I think Rushdie's com-
mentators and Barthes's own work, among other texts, raise:
Are cross-genre writers—feminist or otherwise—committed to
an expressivist theory of writing, faithfully relying on trans-
gressive writing to express their (changing) selves as well as to
change their world? Or are they irrevocably estranged from an
authentic authorial self, their subjectivity construed only in a
phallogocentric discourse neither of their own making nor sub-
ject to their creative control? Are contemporary American femi-
nists who meld poetry and prose, autobiography, literary inter-
pretation, cultural critique, and aesthetic manifesto blending
genres and disciplines for reasons quite different than those
offered by French fashioners of "bricolage"? Where are the over-
laps, where the differences?

Previously I mentioned how Lacanians believe words to be
the death of or "elegy to" the thing, a notion, like Barthes's in
"The Death of the Author," that suggests we become subjects-
in-language only at a cost. If one's subjectivity is constructed
only in and through language, and language is not itself abso-
lute (signifying only in relation, within a system of difference),

neither is the subject absolute, unified, or empowered by language. The author-subject's freedom and integrity are always already threatened. What does it mean then for feminists to challenge the impersonality of academic discourse, with its third-person "they" or "one," or the royal, exclusionary "we," if when we write "I" we erase or are separated from "ourselves"? One answer might be that while in the precarious position of being at once divided from ourselves and constructive of ourselves when we write "I," we are not divided from other writers when we straddle that space. "An identity may be discontinuous [but it is not] therefore alone," Lee Edwards notes in "Self Assertions," an article reviewing new theories of women's autobiographies (8). Or writers with multiple and conflicting identities may find that they are alternately capable and incapable of expressing or constructing that layered self in flux. Thus, there may be several ways of resolving the poststructuralist/feminist alliance/conflict that American feminist Catherine Stimpson describes as an attempt to write on the interleaf between two pages, each espousing different views of language.

In *Where the Meanings Are: Feminism and Cultural Spaces* (1988), a collection of spirited essays, Stimpson addresses the dilemma of feminist literary theorists in the poststructuralist/postmodernist age of Barthes, Foucault, Jacques Derrida, and others. In her introduction, she asks:

> How are we to write on the space of an interleaf between two pre-existing pages? One, the more powerful, the better read, tells of a feminism that uses language to change the moral and material world and to empower women as human agents. The second page, now being inked in, tells of a theory that, like feminism, believes in the potency of language and ideology, of discourse. . . . However, unlike feminists, this theory is agnostic, even atheistic, about language's referential powers and about a human agent's control of those powers. How, on such an interleaf, are we to parse this: "Women are the subjects of the sentence of their lives." (xviii–xix)

Simply asking this question, Stimpson continues, places her book "within the boundaries of post-modernism," "post-modern" being that "tent of a word" (Stimpson's phrase) under which my work, and that of the alchemists I have described, must then tent-atively fall. Stimpson states that poststructuralism gives way to postmodernism as her work's new key word, but she continues to operate in the confluence of several movements all implicated in or impinging on one another, asking as they do analogous questions about discourse, authority, freedom, and form. All can be "tented" under a definition of postmodernism as that which "distrusts the hierarchical, the authoritarian . . . prefers to sense patterns, connections, relationships . . . [and] responds to ironies, ambiguities, open ends, multiple perspectives" (xix).

And yet, just because such a definition overlaps in part with mine of the work of border-crossing feminist poet-critics does not necessarily mean that the latter's writing should or must be subsumed under a postmodern or poststructuralist or reader-response critical tent. Rather, feminist amalgams willingly and unwittingly mix recent and past rhetorical and theoretical trends just as poststructuralist/postmodernist, psychoanalytical, reader-response, or rhetorical theories borrow from feminist ethics and aesthetics. Similarly, my focusing on connections here may be said to demonstrate both the oft-cited notion that, whatever the source, be it biological or historical, "women [are] more capable of affiliation, of psychic fluidity, than men" (Stimpson 126) and the relational power long attributed to the poet, whether male or female. (As Charles Altieri, thinking particularly of Emerson, has said, "What the poet does is make connections, which then allows for a fluidity in one's own life. Poetry is an intensifier and clarifier of relations without any mystique of unity.")

Stimpson's own discourse itself records a confluence: she quotes from Derrida and explores questions of difference(s); like feminist psychoanalytical critics, she employs metaphors of the body and/in language ("language's push of joy") and creates neologisms; she brings autobiography into her criticism, most obviously in "Black Culture/White Teacher" and "On Work"; and she makes special note of Tillie Olsen's voice moving from "elegy to accusation; from lament to anger; from grief to controlled jeremiad" (72) and of Adrienne Rich's "cross[ing] of autobiography with biography, polemic with scholarship, political theory with literary criticism" (142). Her summing up of Rich's work could in many ways apply to her own: "In part, [Rich's] transgressions of genetic conventions are the deconstructive gestures of postmodernism—without much manic play or lucid romps. In greater part, her mingling of 'subjective' and 'objective' genres, advocacy and argument, demonstrates her belief in their inseparability. Her style also emblemizes the position of contemporary, educated women. No longer forced to choose between . . . writing about public or private concerns, women can take on both—at once" (142). Writing on the interleaf may mean just the kind of border crossing I've been attempting, and attempting to advocate, all along.

The words and events that transpired in response to Rushdie's novel and the Ayatollah's order alternately suggest that we might control the sentence of our lives and that we cannot. Rushdie's words, seemingly careening out of his control, changed his status from fiction writer to blasphemer, insurgent, and traitor, at least in Khomeini's eyes and ears. Or rather, words *about* Rushdie made his novel sound too novel for the Iranian dictator of Islamic will(s), who had probably not himself read the work. Yet, despite Rushdie's later apology, neither his new words nor reports about them could redeem him, save him. They seemed then to serve only to reaffirm his antagonists' desire to do him in.

The message or moral is then that words can damn but not redeem. On the other hand, all the words and events—including the reading of Rushdie's damaging words—given in support of Rushdie and in support of freedom of the press, might imply that words *can* save, redeem, and uplift, or at least, that there are still those of us who believe this possible fiction.

There is both consolation and danger in the mutuality I have suggested here between the feminist/poststructuralist alliance/differences and the alliance/differences between Rushdie and his various respondents. (And my impulse to make analogies has the status of a contemporary critical trend among feminists/poststructuralists/poet-critics: we are all seduced by and reduced to analogy, obsessed by meaning-in-relation.) Like Rushdie, feminist writers have been considered blasphemous, their lives or their writing (which is their life, many assert) threatened because of the forms they take, because of the writer's gender, politics, sexuality, race, class, or some combination of them. I think of "self-proclaimed 'post-Christian' radical feminist" Mary Daly being denied promotions at Boston College, a Roman Catholic university (Steinfels A14). I think of Anzaldúa's and Moraga's fearing their family and former communities' reception of them and their works. I think of Margaret Randall, long denied the right to return to the U.S. Russian poets sent to Siberia. Women whose names, and certainly their writing, never surface at all.[5]

Those who can, may write to change what is, but they are caught by what was, whether this be cultural, religious, or discursive regimes. The age of critical/literary elision and alchemy I've been celebrating in one context has dire consequences in another: while I've been touched by writing that intimately connects writer with reader, a writer's life with her words, and one text or one reader with another, I have to be appalled that those who would burn Rushdie's book also mean to burn him, also mean to kill his readers, defenders, interviewers, publishers, librarians, and kin, all considered analogs or co-perpetrators (especially when these supporters, for reasons of solidarity and symbolism, proclaim *themselves* Rushdie's coauthors, or even claim, as many did in full-page advertisements in the *New York Times* and elsewhere, "We are Salman Rushdie.")

It seems ironic and insensitive that while contemporary feminist theorists debate discursive propositions—whether discourse controls us (indeed, is everything) or we can shape it and thus our lives—writers like Rushdie are being manipulated by mass misreadings (both his own misreading of his safety in words and the misreading of Islamic extremists, who, rather than recognizing Rushdie's right of expression, think Rushdie's writing confers retaliatory rights on them). The failure of Rushdie's written apology to lift his death threat suggests that (first) words matter so much they cannot be made (to) unmatter. And if his words (and our invoking of them) are not immaterial, then we deny the death of the author; most of us believe after all (or within our multifarious selves) in the power of language to change and challenge the moral and material world.

Read in yet another context, however, the Rushdie affair may corroborate Foucault's contention that there is no individual author so much as an "author-function," or better, a "transdiscursive" author, the author of an idea or tradition more than a text (153). That is, Rushdie has become the "Rushdie affair," the "Rushdie episode," catch phrases that condense or rewrite Rushdie and his outlawed book into a generalized phenomenon or example—The Censored One. Rushdie is that part of any of us or any society that is transgressive and yet unfairly, perhaps murderously, treated. Rushdie is exiled, set apart—and yet, ironically enough, he is more a part of the polis now than ever he was in "real life" or as a writer with a private practice. In fact, he becomes us ("We are Rushdie"). We read him now as inspiration for our own authority, our own writing, rather than for his authority. We write to say what (and that) the condemned and denied can no longer write with ease.

In fact, more than ever, writers around the world are joining together to fight for and celebrate freedom of the press. U.S. radio broadcasters too, feeling hampered and hemmed in by the new conservatism, have taken out full-page print advertisements to drum up support for an anticensorship campaign. A March 27, 1989, advertisement by Pacifica Radio in the *New York Times* points out:

> It's easy to bash the Ayatollah.
> Especially when you don't have a price on your head.
> It's a little more risky to point out that
> America has its own Ayatollahs—sworn enemies
> of fundamental rights and liberties.
> Especially when your broadcast license is at
> stake.
> But since everybody's coming out against
> censorship, this may be the safest time to do
> so.

As Peter Elbow announced in a talk just two weeks earlier about the growing numbers of people rejecting conservatism in academic discourse, people are "more angry now that there's a whiff of hope" that things might change/are changing. (Of course, the more things change, the more the enemies of left-leaning "political correctness" strive to have them remain the same, but that's another discussion.)

Writing that merges woman, poet, politics, and personal and collective pasts and presents uses as its material, and makes material, the trials and tribulations encountered in the "real world." At the same time, such writing acknowledges the ways discourse always constructs how we are in the world and who we are. It rightly recognizes that words are deeds and yet reveals the gap between words and the deeds our words would detail. "Words are also actions, and actions are a kind of words," Emerson wrote in "The Poet," allowing me to link once again poetic legacy and theory with theories that everything is discourse and that discourse is powerful, whatever the extent to which human agents can control it. Creative-critical amalgams are thus potentially powerful reconcilers of referential, social-constructive, and poststructuralist views of language. Feminist poet-critics imply we are both what is said and what we say, how we are spoken and how we speak in response. Even in light of contemporary theories of discourse, feminist poet-critics persist in writing performatively, anew, attempting to wrest self-determined identities from predetermined contexts, images, idioms, ideologies.[6] And those selves (re)constructed and (re)created in language have longevity.

Thus, even if we believe we are subject to a subjectivity not our own—constructed instead in and by language, never free from/within the regime, the cultural syntax into which we are born—at least we can commune and communicate with others similarly wrought and wrestling. We can create a collaborative pastiche of our lives and words, both individually and collectively. As Rushdie does in his novel, authors like Gloria Anzaldúa can rely on old forms, old iconography—the Aztecan mosaic, for example—to look back as well as forward, to re-create or re-present one's heritage at the same time as revise it, creating it and oneself differently, anew. It is as if we are saying, I have the past but it doesn't have me. We can sidestep the question of controlling discourse (note the grammatical ambiguity of the phrase). Through textual crossings, feminist writers faithfully, if naïvely, continue to try to shake up old belief systems, old discourse conventions, despite the threat of physical, spiritual, or authorial excommunication or death.

More Analogs, Precedents, Parallels, Examples

In a host of ways, genres are becoming blurred. It is worth quoting Geertz: "The present jumbling of varieties of discourse has grown to the point where it is becoming difficult either to label authors (What is Foucault—historian, philosopher, political theorist? . . .) or to classify works. . . . It is a phenomenon general enough and distinctive enough to suggest that what we are seeing is not just another redrawing of the cultural map . . . but an alteration of the principles of mapping."
> Peter Elbow, "Reflections on Academic Discourse"

Certainly, American feminists do not have to be original in everything. They borrow texts and impulses from their sisters and brothers, their continental coworkers, their ancestors. As Julia Kristeva claims, "Every text takes shape as a mosaic of citations, every text is the absorption and transformation of other texts" (*Semiotike,* quoted in Bruss 64–65). Feminist poet-critics like Susan Griffin, Adrienne Rich, Marge Piercy, Gloria Anzaldúa, Cherrie Moraga, or Louise Bernikow draw on personal, institutional, literary-critical, and poetic history along with current events for their trans-generic inspiration. They share what's in the air. Generic or disciplinary border crossing is evidently the subject or hallmark of many recent works by writers who are not necessarily American women or poets or lesbians or members of ethnic, racial, or religious minorities or members of the working class. As a brief inventory will show, analogous or alternative instances of cross- or blurred-genre texts have been produced and theorized by deconstructors, French psychoanalytic critics, reader-response critics, and composition teachers, not to mention past poet-critics from Sir Philip Sidney and Walt Whitman to Gertrude Stein and Charles Olson (and anthropologists such as Clifford Geertz, James Clifford, and George E. Marcus).

Judith Fetterley has argued that nineteenth-century American women writers may have done their best work in nontraditional genres rather than, for example, the novel. In prose that may itself be described as cross-genre, a blend of the personal and academic, she reasons that such forms as the letter, the sketch, the personal essay, the newspaper column, and short fiction were less likely to be interfered with than the "big" form, the novel. "Writers who wished to . . . experiment with artistic form might well have chosen to work in genres less formalized, less pretentious, less predetermined, and therefore more open, fluid, and malleable to their uses" (14). The American women writers whose works Fetterley includes in her anthology *Provisions* might be said to offer a legacy of not-genres[7]—anomalous genres, cross-genres—to twentieth-century women writers. The images and realities of the domestic sewing circle and U.S. westward expansion may have provided some border-crossing form and content, as I mention in chapter 2, and the home arts of quilting and gardening, of making do with little, may have provided still more methods and metaphors for contemporary feminist poet-critics, as I argue in chapter 4.

For white feminist poet-critics as well as feminists of color, a crucial nineteenth-century legacy is that of the slave narrative, where literacy and liberty are inextricably linked. Reading and writing enabled one to orchestrate an escape; to read the Bible or other inspirational, identity-constituting texts (such as *The Columbian Orator,* a book of rhetoric that offered Frederick Douglass the example of a man arguing deftly against slavery); to communicate with relatives; to be able to publish, for money and to further the abolitionist cause, one's story. The world-famous *Narrative of the Life of Frederick Douglass* (1845), for example, provides one model for a literature of protest. It seems to say, Here's my (humble) story, but that's not even the worst of it; slavery clearly makes a beast of both master and slave, especially when the slave is not allowed the light of literacy. Providing another early model for the feminist-critical exhortative and testimonial modes, Harriet Jacob's *Incidents in the Life of a Slave Girl* (1861) portrays male as well as white domination and sexual intimidation. As Henry Louis Gates, Jr., points out, Jacobs "appeals directly to a female readership . . . by selecting as one of her epigraphs Isaiah 22:9: 'Rise up! ye women that are at ease! Hear my voice, ye careless daughters!'" (xviii).

These personal/political/religious narratives, intended to "leave *on record* 'humble testimony' to be read by 'succeeding generations,'" in turn grew out of not only dramatic oral testimonies complete with shows of scars from the lash but also Puritan confessional accounts and Methodist conversion narratives (particularly in their pious tones and moral reflections), according to critic Houston Baker (12). Much has been written, especially by Gates and Baker, on the theory that African-American literature has been autobiographical since its inception (and thus, such literature inevitably works its influence on contemporary feminist autobiographical-critical amalgams from those of Alice Walker to those of Adrienne Rich). Moreover, Rich reminds us that when we read Audre Lorde or Barbara Smith (or June Jordan, Michelle Cliff, Alice Walker, and more, I would add), we need to understand that "the intellectual roots of this feminist theory are not [I would say not only] white liberalism or white Euro-American feminism, but the analyses of Afro-American experience articulated by Sojourner Truth, W. E. B. Du Bois, Ida B. Wells-Barnett, . . . Malcolm X, Lorraine Hansberry. . . . Black feminism . . . is an organic development of the Black movements and philosophies of the past, their practice and their printed writings" (*BBP* 231).

It should be no surprise that the testimonial rhetoric of feminist consciousness-raising sessions and the interdisciplinary reading, thinking, and writing of Women's Studies programs have also provided feminist poet-critics a large measure of their com-

positional methodology and motivation. The feminist move-
ments in America (including early abolitionist and suffragist
movements) have always relied on women sharing their stor-
ies—of isolation, oppression, exclusion, silence, abuse, and
poverty, or friendship, companionship, sexual relations, and
children. According to Joel Myerson, feminist Margaret Fuller
(1810–1850), editor of the Transcendentalist journal *The Dial*,
"supported herself by holding 'Conversations' for women on top-
ics such as poetry, ethics, Greek mythology or . . . other sub-
jects. . . . She saw herself as a catalyst for the women in her
groups, and . . . she attempted to guide and draw out partici-
pants, to force them to realize the potential in themselves. . . .
The 'Conversations' anticipate the later organization of wom-
en's literary clubs and other efforts aimed at the self-develop-
ment of women" (1581). Women have long had to find their own
spheres and discourse.

Feminism "aims for individual freedoms by mobilizing sex
solidarity," explains Nancy F. Cott in *What is Feminism?* "It ac-
knowledges diversity among women while positing that women
recognize their unity" (49). In the early 1970s, women in con-
sciousness-raising groups (a more radical version of Fuller's
'Conversations,' we might say) theorized collaboratively out of
their personal experiences as members of the "other" sex or
their double (or triple) oppression as members of ethnic or racial
minorities or as members of the (economic) underclasses.[8] Thus
Marge Piercy acknowledges her reliance on group work when
she asserts, "I am not able to make the distinction between the
personal and the political that seems to come easily to people
who have not lived their lives involved in struggle and *group
practice*" (*PCB* 183; emphasis mine). Piercy further confides,
in "Looking at Myself: A Study in Focused Myopia," "I am
conscious in my poems of exploring the experience of being a
woman in this society. I am consciously a feminist working with,
by, and for other women. I feel an identity too with other people
in struggle" (*PCB* 201). And in her essay describing Adrienne
Rich's legacies to women writers, she quotes one of the Rich
practices she herself most adopts: "'I believe increasingly that
only the willingness to share private and sometimes painful

experience can enable women to create a collective description of the world which will be truly ours'"(*PCB* 269). Corroborating the notion that contemporary American women's aesthetics and rhetoric derive in part from traditional female forms (also deemed "nontraditional" literature), Piercy adds that Rich has accomplished this kind of sharing of private experience through writing based on "her old journals, her memories" (269).

Women's Studies programs began (and in many places, still exist) as Women's Studies committees, minors, advisory boards, or feminist colloquia rather than an academic major or a department with a reliable budget, tenure lines, and so forth. These committees brought together first women faculty, then women students (and finally the new "other" sex as well), from a variety of departments spanning the humanities, social sciences, and natural and physical sciences, as well as mathematics: as "outsiders in the sacred grove, the women of academe"[9] thought disciplinary divisions to be as arbitrary or potentially dangerous as divisions by sex, class, race, sexual preference, physical ability, and so forth. (I think again of Adrienne Rich's *Of Woman Born,* with its mix of literary and cultural analyses, anthropology, myth studies, autobiography, and philosophy, with yet other disciplinary discourses, or of Griffin's *Woman and Nature* or *Made from This Earth,* Gallop's *Thinking Through the Body,* Anzaldúa's *Borderlands/La Frontera,* Moraga's *Loving in the War Years,* Kingston's *Woman Warrior* and *China Men,* and other texts too numerous to explore in this study, including Paula Gunn Allen's *Sacred Hoop,* Frye's *Politics of Reality,* Grahn's *Highest Apple,* Lorde's *Sister Outsider,* and Rachel Blau DuPlessis's *Pink Guitar.*)

Still another set of antecedents for generic and private-public blurring and bending, for renovating conventions, comes, as I have said, from American poetic history. I borrow Shirley Brice Heath's compact summary of this kind of legacy:

> The move of authors away from the established forms and genres of Great Britain and the continent in the 1830s, coupled with Transcendentalist debates over inspiration and craftsmanship

in writing, led off the first serious American attention to language per se. Emerson considered . . . the source of convention or "laws" in language, the extent to which "ordinary speech" could (and should) be written. . . . Edgar Allen Poe . . . proposed that grammar be a descriptive analysis of language, not an adaptation of the rules of Latin and Greek. In many ways, his views anticipate . . . modernist poets: he rejected some established patterns of English meter and verse and argued instead for the natural rhythms of speech. "The language of common speech" was a topic addressed . . . by Walt Whitman, Mark Twain . . . Emily Dickinson . . . Gertrude Stein, Wallace Stevens, and William Carlos Williams.[10]

Since the 1950s, various American literary rebellions have fought against prior forms, aesthetics and traditions. Poets have not only lashed out against "traditional" forms, but have also chosen as their topics private anguish, individual mental journeys. ("Being Literate in America: A Sociohistorical Perspective" 5–6)

Heath even more specifically conjoins past poets with recent literary theorists in her essay "Literacy and Language Change." She sees William Carlos Williams, "physician, poet, novelist, and essayist" (in short, poet-critic), as someone whose "approaches to language foreshadow those of current literary theorists, ranging from reader-response proponents to deconstructionists." Williams tries "(as Gertrude Stein had also done) to create in written form the language of oral debate as well as the dialogic argumentation of inner voices of the writer reflecting uncertainty, idea association, and image extension" (287). Since so many of the women poet-critics I discuss in chapters 1, 2, and 4 wrote personal poems of "private anguish" or "individual mental journeys" before turning to prose (Rich, Piercy, Griffin, Gallagher), their prose is inevitably informed by such journeys and journalizing. Like Williams and Stein, contemporary feminist poet-critics in many ways both foreshadow and embody reader-response and other contemporary theories.

Still other poet-critics and experimental or markedly autobiographical novelists provide antecedents and parallels to contemporary feminist poet-critics. I have noted earlier that, in

Robert Von Hallberg's view, American poet-critics since 1945—
Robert Hass, Robert Pinsky, Randall Jarrell, Donald Hall, J. V.
Cunningham, and Howard Nemerov among them—are (as I
also maintain about feminist poet-critics) "more direct about
stating premises than academic critics" (285), more likely to
treat criticism as an "improvisatory art, full of inconsistencies"
(288). These writers rarely emphasize issues of gender, race, or
class, however, as feminist poet-critics do. Later in his chapter,
however, Von Hallberg notes that historically, poet-critics have
written about contemporary political as well as literary issues,
and he cites recent poet-critics who "have used critical prose to
advocate political objectives": "They [Imamu Amiri Baraka,
Wendell Berry, Denise Levertov, Adrienne Rich, and Kenneth
Rexroth] have written on racism, strip-mining, nuclear disar-
mament, women's rights" (294). In fact, whenever I mention my
project to friends and colleagues, they are quick to volunteer the
names of still other writers who blend genres, experiment with
the personal voice, or just talk about related phenomena.

They offer me the likes of James Joyce, David Antin, Jean
Toomer, Vladimir Nabokov, Vikram Seth, Don DeLillo, Roland
Barthes, Jacques Derrida, Frantz Fanon, Monique Wittig, and
Julia Kristeva, not to mention all the writers in the *Poets on
Poetry* series published by the University of Michigan Press. I
have argued that American feminist poet-critics' versions of
cross-genre writing are frequently different both in kind and
intent—more self-disclosingly metadiscursive, personal, acces-
sible, informal, and homegrown—though they are often sim-
ilarly engaged in theorizing about language or social and in-
stitutional change. Mary DeShazer describes well a contrast
between male and female poet-critics through the examples of
essays by Adrienne Rich and T. S. Eliot. In "Creation and Rela-
tion: Teaching Essays by Adrienne Rich and T. S. Eliot," De-
Shazer notes that in "When We Dead Awaken: Writing as Re-
Vision," Rich speaks against the impersonal artist that T. S.
Eliot calls for in his essay "Tradition and the Individual Tal-
ent." Rich's essay doesn't turn on the key term *tradition* as
Eliot's does, and Eliot's own prose style is "masculinist"— "for-
mal, detached, pontifical," full of "absolute assertions"—while

Rich's style is "informal, vulnerable . . . forthright" (115–18). Rich both practices and praises subjectivity over the allegiance to objectivity, tradition, and the "patriarchal" aesthetic one finds in Eliot (118); she believes that the best writing by women today challenges this philosophy of dehumanization, and it is "subjective, engaged, attached" (115).

And yet, I would agree that more and more male writers are endorsing the "female mode" of rhetoric, offering a subjective, personal, fluid, or interactive compositional legacy. For example, while the great majority of essays submitted to and included in *The Intimate Critique: Autobiographical Literary Criticism*— an essay collection devoted to "'everyday' literary criticism written in nontraditional forms: feminine, personal, narrative, mixed-genre, interactive, or subjective, and so on"—are by women writers, my co-editors and I also include essays by three male writers.[11] Autobiographical-critical hybrids (though again, not all as informal, vulnerable, forthright, or home-grown as those by the feminist poet-critics I mainly celebrate) are springing up more and more at the crossroads of several powerful recent movements and theories.

Note the obvious overlaps in the vocabulary of autobiographical, feminist, composition, reader-response, and poststructuralist theorists in the following assertions along with the epigraphs at the beginning of the chapter. All advocate or announce the blurring of the border between writer and reader, critic and creative artist.

"[Structuralism's] conception of writing . . . as an amalgam of personal and cultural 'codes' draws no sharp distinction between literature and composition," suggests William Stull, who adds, "As [reader-response critic] Steven Mailloux has argued, reader-response criticism and recent work in composition have proved highly compatible" (137). Similarly, according to (poststructuralist) Ihab Hassan, "In desiring, in reading, in making, the critic acts out his [*sic*] autobiography, compounded of many selves" (433). Composition theorists Bruce Peterson, Mariolina Salvatori, Keith Fort, Charles Moran, and Anthony Petrosky, among others—in addition to reader-response theorists from Louise Rosenblatt through David Bleich, Nancy Jo Hoffman, and Elizabeth Flynn—call for students to write personal "response statements" to literature or otherwise to close the gap between reader and writer, giving the reader-writer a status akin to that of published author/published text.[12] As Flynn attests, "Feminist inquiry and composition studies have much in common" (424). Hoffman describes a classroom community of women who together define criticism as a mediation between poetry and their lives; they see that "the poem is an arena into which we enter to change ourselves and each other" (52).

In her 1938 text reissued in 1976, *Literature as Exploration,* early reader-response critic Rosenblatt asserted that "the reader counts for at least as much as the book or poem itself . . . through books, the reader may explore his [*sic*] own nature" and "just as the author is creative, selective, so the reader also is creative" (42). Just as I do, Humm acknowledges Rosenblatt's usefulness for the feminist writerly reader: "Although not a programmatic feminist (evident in her designation of the reader as 'he'), Rosenblatt is helpful to feminism in her instrumental use of criticism. She has extended her critique of the reading process to define aesthetic choice as the prerogative of the reader not the writer" (108). Contemporary critics David Bleich and Norman Holland (see "Transactive Teaching"), to name but two, draw on Rosenblatt in their notion of "subjective criticism" (Bleich's term and the title of one of his books), in which readers' feelings and memories when reading literature are "negotiated" in group discussion. Salvatori blends Rosenblatt and (reception theorist) Wolfgang Iser when she reiterates Rosenblatt's idea that literature ought to be taught "as a way of exploring, understanding, reflecting on the strategies by which readers—all readers—generate meanings in the act of reading" (659) and Iser's that "central to the act of every literary work is the interaction between its structure and its recipient" (quoted in Salvatori 660).

In truth, however, most of these teacher-theorists and others like them are unlikely to write as subjectively, associatively, autobiographically, or creatively as they theorize other readers'

(notably students') writing might fruitfully do.[13] In this re-
gard, as well as in their "creative-reader" vocabulary, they re-
semble most commentators on poststructuralist critics. Murray
Krieger, for example, in an article providing an impersonal
overview, observes that these critics in their "most forceful pos-
ture . . . would do away with any distinction among modes of
discourse, indeed . . . even the distinction between criticism and
the poem which is its object" (29). English Marxist critic Terry
Eagleton concludes "there is no clear division for poststructur-
alism between 'criticism' and 'creation': both are subsumed into
'writing' as such" (139), while his own writing is rather conven-
tionally ordered and impersonal. For American psychoanalytic
critic Harold Bloom, criticism is just as much a form of poetry as
poems are implicitly literary criticism of other poems (Eagleton
185).

While these commentators and poststructuralist, reader-
response and psychoanalytical critics themselves do not neces-
sarily write in a way most would consider either creative or
deeply personal, their programs do resemble American feminist
poet-critics' in their contemplation of the powers of discourse;
their frequent insistence on eliding the categories or discourses
of criticism and creative writing, autobiography and analysis;
their willingness to read or deconstruct events and artifacts of
popular culture along with texts more traditionally considered
literary[14]; and their sometime interest in the social construc-
tion of the psychological subject.

I make another analogy in likening Krieger's description
of the poststructuralist/deconstructionist posture (adopted by
such diverse writers as Lévi-Strauss, Lacan, Foucault, Derrida,
and Barthes) to the practice of feminist poet-critics whose crit-
icism is as poetic as their poetry is critical. Krieger asserts that
such a posture would "deny that criticism serves, as a secondary
and derivative art, the primary art of poetry. Instead it would
see them both, with all their sister disciplines, sharing—as
coordinates and equals—the common realm of *écriture*" (29).
Krieger then delights in pointing out the irony in this contem-
porary penchant for analogy or affinity in an age of supposed
deference to difference: "However favorable our attitude toward

interdisciplinary study may be . . . this procedure may well sug-
gest too easy and undifferentiated a series of analogies (or
rather homologies), especially—we should add—for a theory
based on the doctrine of difference" (29).

Indeed it is true that contemporary critics intrigued by the
implications of Saussure and structuralism—that nothing has
meaning of itself but only in a system of difference—have an
affinity for the analogy. There's a further lovely irony in what
Krieger oxymoronically calls "a monolithic principle of differ-
entiation": the principle of *difference* is what makes systems,
makes texts, so *similar.* A first dictionary definition of *system* is
that of unity in diversity. Analogies operate in that systematiz-
ing spirit: like metaphors and similes, they are most pleasur-
able when most surprising, when they are torn by the tension or
oscillation of sameness (unity) and difference (diversity, diver-
gency). As the poet Robert Frost put it, "All metaphor breaks
down somewhere. That is the beauty of it. It is touch and go with
the metaphor. . . . You don't know how much you can get out of it
and when it will cease to yield." He went on, "You have to live
with it long enough to see where it is going" (1029).

Of course, the analogies I have been making break down. Those
writers with the extreme dream of a common language believe
meaning resides in relations with people, not within a linguistic
system of difference, and they both proclaim and enact their
refusal to separate poet and critic, private and public lives and
language. They don't seek an institutional solution, though
they seek to change the academic institution as we now know it.
On the other hand, those wholly convinced that everything is
discourse come to democracy by default, or through a back door:
"The absence of the transcendental signified extends the do-
main and the interplay of signification ad infinitum," Derrida
announced in 1966; thus (br)other continental critics were led
to conclude that the difference between literature and criticism
was delusive (DeMan 33). This is all to say that for many femi-
nist, reader-response, and compositionist critics, the authority
of primary texts (not to mention canonical and conventional
texts) is questioned in the name of empowerment and engage-

ment (on the part of students-and-readers-become-writers), while for the antihumanist deconstructionists, textual authority is played upon only in the name of the infinite play of signification.

And yet, the urge to analogize, to mediate, persists. Though not, strictly speaking, a poet-critic,[15] Jane Gallop sees connections too in asserting that her own mixture of the theoretical and autobiographical was preceded—and inspired—by the various blends offered up by psychoanalyst Freud, feminist poet-critic Rich, and poststructuralist Barthes. As I allude to in the previous chapter, Gallop sees an analogy between "two non-aligned intellectual movements of the seventies—American feminism and post-structuralism—in the unusual combination of autobiography and theory" practiced by Rich and Barthes. Both writers blur the boundary between scholar and writer, public and private, autobiography and scholarship (4). And Helen Vendler decrees that Barthes stands "for the blurring of models, for many-sided meanings, for the oscillation of values, for metamorphosis" (69). Gallop particularly focuses on analogy (and *anal*ogy) as central to Freud and thus to her own feminist/psychoanalytical/autobiographical approach to (interdisciplinary) literature in the poststructuralist age.

In "The Anal Body," Gallop notes that while Freud saw analysis as a reconstruction of "some ancient edifice that has been destroyed and buried," or possibly as an hallucination, Gallop herself is convinced that "the analyst produces literary texts 'according to the desire of his [*sic*] imagination'" (*Thinking Through the Body* 29). We are all three analysts here. As I see it, Gallop produces a literary text, one describing how Freud's work can be read as a literary text, in fact, "according to the desire of [her] imagination." In the previous chapter, I also link Freud's life and text to mine; in this chapter, I cannot help finding Gallop's burrowing into and borrowing from, among others, Freud, Barthes, Rich, Foucault, and Lacan analogous to my own work—and to the work of other contemporary poet-critics—as well.

*

To make a metaphor is to make a fuss, and I am a poet,
though it seems that is something one cannot claim for one-
self; anyway, I write poetry. I am enough of them, my kind
family, to be repelled by the significance of things, to find
poetry, with its tendency to make connections and to break
the barriers between past and present, embarrassing.
                    Patricia Hampl, *A Romantic Education*

What do I as a feminist gain (or lose) by finding personal, alchemical writing (theorized) among outsiders to both feminism and America? I find it useful—and pleasurable—to acknowledge the different yet somehow analogous theories of, and homage to, the collage text or the elision of literature and criticism, however much this move undercuts my larger, previous move of differentiating feminist poet-critics from other critics and poet-critics. Making or seeing these connections allows me to step back a moment from the ways in which men and women, American and French feminists, and individual American feminist poet-critics write—and conceive of their writing—differently. Further, the feminists' work I celebrate and seek to emulate is based, as poetry is, on the tension between differentiating and assimilating, sharing and separating.

For example, Cherrie Moraga wants to write in her cultural idiom yet knows she must be, and is, separate in her unconventional lesbianism, her feminism, her writing. Maxine Hong Kingston both accepts and rejects her mother and her prohibitions. Adrienne Rich gains power from poetically resurrecting Marie Curie but ultimately must, unlike Curie, refuse to "deny her wounds." And Alice Walker, though she plants flowers in the tradition of her mother, is unlike her mother in writing about them. Walker is able to create in a room of her own, in economic ease relative to her mother, freed by the profits of best-selling books and cash retainers from magazines.

Just as I bring Frost (no feminist) to bear on my theories of analogies and feminist poet-critics, all poets tend toward connections, create rich intertexts. They join, as Patricia Hampl notes above, past and present, line and (enjambed or rhymed) line, alliterated words, vehicle and tenor, and the circumstances of vehicle and that of tenor, of poet and reader, of one poet and another. Even when the theme of a poem is separation, lines may still enjamb, or, if they do graphically depict separation, on another level the lines "connect" in a kind of visual onomatopoeia with the theme—as they do in the Anzaldúa poem discussed in the previous chapter.

In "The Evening News," for example, Audre Lorde connects herself with Winnie Mandela and her anti-apartheid cause by figuratively touching Mandela with her fingers, those fingers that have literally wrought the connecting lines:

> Winnie Mandela I am feeling your face
> with pain of my crippled fingers
> our children are escaping their births
> on the streets of Soweto and Brooklyn.

Lorde underscores her attempt at physical, literal connection with alliteration ("feeling," "face," "fingers"; "births," "Brooklyn") and her merging, mapping together the streets of Soweto and Brooklyn. To cite another example, Rich's line "Any woman's death diminishes me" ("From an Old House in America," *FD* 222) asserts Rich's connection both with other women and with other poets, particularly John Donne—who wrote, in the poetic prose of a "Meditation" (XVII), "Any man's death diminishes me because I am involved in mankind, and therefore never send to know for whom the bell tolls; it tolls for thee." Much of the strength of Rich's line, the last of her poem, resides in its readers knowing Donne, recognizing the old line even as Rich seeks here and elsewhere to rewrite history, including poetic history, including her own.

Gallop describes the critic-theorist's mode of knowledge as that of categorizing and the poet's as a sensitivity to what is violated by such categories (3). Hampl's words seem to elaborate upon this: "Even in our country where poetry is not read, as we're always told, the poet symbolizes the personal voice" (219). The *poet-critic*, be it Barthes or Rich, Gallop or Lorde, can resist neither categorizing nor connecting. When I describe analogies as both "useful" and "pleasurable," I am saying I find analogies the site of both categorizing/analyzing and collaborating/creating. Again, we need a blend of at least two kinds of discourses: the analytical and the experiential.

As I have argued with regard to feminist writers, Geoffrey Hartman claims there is at work a fusion of creation with criticism in the writings of contemporary critics in general. In his much reproduced "Literary Commentary as Literature," Hartman asserts that the school of Derrida "confronts us with a substantial problem, What are the proper relations between the 'critical' and 'creative' activities, or between 'primary' and 'secondary' texts?" (345). He is careful to acknowledge that Eliot and Arnold, though (to him) prototypes of the creative artist-critic, are not role models for Derrida; Derrida is reputedly "no poet or even man of letters in the tradition of Mallarmé, Valery, Malraux, Arnold, and Eliot." Yet, Hartman continues, the "new philosophic criticism has a scope that . . . seems to stand in a complex and even *crossover* relation to both art and philosophy" (346; emphasis mine). The result is a "medley of insight and idiosyncratic self-assertion" (348–49).

In *The Fate of Reading and Other Essays,* Hartman sums up, "We have entered an era that can challenge even the priority of the literary to literary-critical texts" (18). While I'm not at all convinced that feminist poet-critics give their literary-critical texts priority over others'—or their own—literary texts (because this assumes both a clear distinction between the two types of texts and a desire for domination), I do see feminist poet-critics (along with some reader-response and composition theorists or their students) bending and allying genres and discourses. They do resemble Derrida in not modeling themselves on Eliot or Arnold, but unlike Derrida, they are in fact usually poets and women "of letters" as well as critical theorists.[16]

Helen Vendler observes the changes of tone in poet Dave Smith's critical writing and Robert Von Hallberg's occasional departure from a style of "academic distance" to a mix of the "formal with the vulgar" (28). She sees such mutability as a "sign that criticism assuming an authoritarian and impersonal voice . . . is being challenged in a revealing, awkward, and morally hortatory American style, confiding and hectoring at once" (41). In his 1989 talk "Problematics," Peter Elbow notes that while "many academics are more nervous about changes in discourse than changes in content," the notion of a unitary academic discourse is of course illusory. He calls for "more voices, more kinds of voices, more discourse." Moreover, he demonstrates such polyvocality himself, weaving from a witty discourse of lists and reasons—we should teach other writing along with the academic because "life is long and college is short" and "non-academic writing is at least as practical as academic writing, given a student's whole life"—to expressive discourse, a letter to another composition theorist on the platform, David Bartholomae.

Vincent Leitch, in "The Book of Deconstructive Criticism," speaks of the "critical text beginning to break up," noting that "the borders between the literary text are giving way. And metatexts on critical texts are springing up everywhere . . . criticism is becoming libidinal: a self indulgent, yet earnest, joy of reading and writing" (137)—ideas with which we are by now familiar. Despite all the theories of an absent self, of Foucault's author function rather than an author, Leitch forgets and gives himself authority (perhaps no surprise in a text with such an authoritative title), in fact celebrates the self, by suggesting writing become more *self*-indulgent. He certainly shares the feminist-poetical spirit of linguistic rebellion when he announces, "The genre of the journal article presents us overly confining limits; it needs to be threatened" (133).

While from nearly every recent school or type of literary criticism there seems to be at least one spokesperson who calls for or identifies increasing informality and intimacy, only feminist poet-critics so widely weave together poetry, autobiography, testimony, literary interpretation, and politics with women's so-called private genres (diary, letter), all bearing on and bearing out issues of gender, race, class, and sexuality. Their metadiscourse is personal in its details while the metadiscourse of male (post)structuralists rarely incorporates such corporeal particularity as can be discerned from titles such as

Gallop's *Thinking Through the Body,* Nancy Mairs's "On Being a Cripple" or *Remembering the Bone House,* Audre Lorde's *Cancer Journals,* Alice Walker's "One Child of One's Own" (*MG*), Marge Piercy's "Looking at Myself: A Study in Focused Myopia" (*PCB*), or Rich's *Of Woman Born.*

To take but one example in a bit more detail: in her first book of autobiographical essays, *Plaintext* (1986), Mairs explains that, as a victim of multiple sclerosis (MS), she calls herself a cripple rather than handicapped or disabled perhaps because she wants people to wince at the word, at her, to see her "as a tough customer, one to whom the fates/gods/viruses have not been kind, but who can face the brutal truth of her existence squarely" (9). Along with her MS and also agoraphobia, Mairs is indeed frank about, to summarize via several of her own apt essay titles, "touching by accident," "being a scientific booby," "not liking sex," "loving men," and "living behind bars" (in a Met State mental ward, where she committed herself after "being in a state of panic so overwhelming that [she] had lost all control over it" [126]). Mairs uses her body-specific experiences to think through her body to reach some generalizations and to wrangle with others. After her stay at Met State, Mairs concludes that perhaps "the standards of social, moral, and emotional health in a patriarchal society are so set . . . that for a woman sickness may be instrinsic to her existence" (141). And, expanding upon and challenging her psychotherapist's diagnosis (that her life became troubled when men entered it), Mairs theorizes that her "life became troubled, not when individual men entered it, but when [she] emerged from the long undifferentiated dream of [her] female-supported childhood into the Real/Male World, an environment defined and dominated by the masculine principles of effectiveness, power, and success, an environment containing a ready-made niche for [her] which happened to be the wrong size and shape" (141). Attracted to such feminist theorists as Chodorow and Nancy Friday, Mairs tests out their hypotheses in her own physical and emotional house, commenting, "All the analyses I've read of mother-daughter relationships fail to account for my experience of [her daughter's] power in our mutual life" (69).

Further, in *Remembering the Bone House: An Erotics of Place and Space* (1989), Mairs takes Hélène Cixous's abstraction of "Women"—"Women haven't had eyes for themselves. They haven't gone exploring in their house. Their sex still frightens them. Their bodies, which they haven't dared enjoy, have been colonized" ("Sorties," quoted in Mairs 7)—and internalizes it, puts it in the first person before going on not only to analyze cultural politics but to invite others into her writing, to their own writing and dreaming. Writing essays about the houses/bodily experiences "where I once lived and where, time collapsing through dreams, I continue to live today" enables Mairs to "return to them, reenter them, in order to discover the relationships they bear to my own erotic development and thus perhaps—because I'm ever aware of myself as a cultural, not merely personal, construct—to feminine erotic development in general" (7). In the final paragraph to "The Way In," Mairs expresses clearly her desire to have her readers cross not only the border/"threshold" of her house and life but to encourage others to do their own crossings: "Think, for example, of your houses: the one you live in now, if you have one, and the ones you have inhabited before. I am writing a book about your houses. You have never lived in a yellow house on the coast of Maine? No matter. . . . If I do my job, the book I write vanishes before your eyes. I invite you into the house of my past, and the threshold you cross leads to your own" (11).

Except for perhaps Barthes, Hélène Cixous, and Luce Irigaray,[17] continental critics (especially male critics), though they may experiment, pun, parody, resist old voices, do not make a point of theorizing out of a personal history made accessible to the reader. If they are metadiscursive, they talk about everything being discourse, but they do not consistently state directly why they chose the form and voice of a given text. They give or disclose little of themselves or their motives. Unlike American feminist poet-critics, their goals are generally not self-disclosure, comfort, warmth, and intimacy with the reader, but instead disruption and "distanciation." (Identification is the opposite of distanciation, an almost onomatopoetic term I first encountered in Deborah Gordon's "Writing Culture, Writing

Feminism: The Poetics and Politics of Experimental Ethnography").

What is especially inviting and new about a feminist (and psychoanalytical critic) like Gallop, for example, is her use of autobiographical details in an otherwise highly theoretical, abstract, and idiosyncratic text. A self-disclosure statement explains: "I found myself adding autobiographical bits not only, I hope, because I tend toward exhibitionism but, more important, because at times I think through autobiography: that is to say, the chain of associations that I am pursuing in my reading passes through things that happened to me" (4). Even so, Gallop's metadiscourse about her self-disclosures is not as voluminous as, say, Rich's or Griffin's or Bernikow's. In *Made from This Earth,* Griffin brings to the fore, as in her book's title, the modes and sources of her writing. As I discuss in the next chapter, Griffin shares in rapid succession such autobiographical bits as, "The discovery of my own voice as a writer occurred simultaneously with my entrance into the feminist" (*MFE* 187); "I have always written out of the experience of my own life, beginning with acutely personal feelings" (3), with "the form of these notes themselves allowing this kind of association and the formal essay as a kind violence, a kind of mutilating plastic surgery to the real process of thought" (225). Griffin shares the contemporary preoccupation with discourse theory, but she finds and features primarily her own (and) feminist discourse.

Bernikow's *Among Women* implies by its very title a rhetoric of engagement or relation. Bernikow situates herself among the authors and characters of the books she reads and the life she lives. She brings "a poet's voice and a scholar's mind to the associations women forge among themselves," according to her book's jacket. A poet (like Griffin, Walker, Rich, Lorde, Piercy, and Mairs, but not Hartman, Bloom, Leitch, Krieger, or Vendler), Bernikow has long been used to writing in a nondominant form; she has been used to making connections, again that fundamental activity of poetry—whether it is finding resemblances between things and sounds or relations between the poet and her subject.

Bernikow begins in the manner of the predominant modern lyric, autobiographically, in a homey setting (as I feel inclined to do, especially in my Afterwords below): "I was sitting at a table on a cloudy day. The table was stacked with books." She muses about women's friendships in novels or their lack, continuing a feminist-collaborative tradition begun with Virginia Woolf in *A Room of One's Own* and reaffirmed in Rich's "Conditions for Work," which quotes Woolf directly: "If Chloe liked Olivia . . ." Each chapter following Bernikow's introduction shares the metadiscursive, autobiographical (often confessional) mode, the immediacy of lyric: "I am writing an essay about Cinderella, spending mornings at the typewriter" (35). In order to analyze and repudiate the women-as-enemies motif of "Cinderella," Bernikow relates to her readers her early exposure to the Disney movie before moving back to texts (such as Perrault's version of the Cinderella tale). She ends with an anecdote about two friends with whom she habitually shares her writing, thankfully concluding, "We are not the terrible stepsisters" (38). It strikes me that Bernikow is asking her readers to join her writing group, we who begin to be a kind of Chloe liking an Olivia; we are also not the terrible stepsisters.

Bernikow repeatedly orchestrates quick scene shifts, with white space instead of logic-words such as *since, however,* and *consequently* serving as transitions. Everything connects. Her essays shift from memory to the present, from text to the outside world, as she moves from chapters about mothers and daughters, sisters, friends, lovers, to conflict and race. The subject matter itself sets this book apart from mainstream literary criticism, but her form does that too. She obfuscates boundaries in her version of the female mode. Jean Kennard's notion in "Personally Speaking: Feminist Critics and the Community of Readers" that the form of feminist essays challenges the critical canon only slightly by habitually beginning with a personal anecdote before launching into conventional (distant, abstract, reasoned) rhetoric is refuted by Bernikow's rhetorical mode throughout *Among Women,* which parallels the description she gives of talking with a woman friend: "The talk was intimate and non-linear, moving from books to people, literature to life, mixing domestic with philosophic quickly, with few bridges. There was an interplay of mothering . . . a certain solicitude and hint of reassurance. We were personal. And physical" (4). The form of her work echoes that of her content. When she observes, for example, that she lives at a turning point, that there are more books than before in which women tell the truth about their lives, she demonstrates precisely this, writing as she does about her troubles and relations with her mother, sister, lovers, and friends, implicitly inviting readers to write their own texts into her own.

In "Mothers and Daughters: Blood, Blood and Love," Bernikow uses literature and literary lives, such as Toni Morrison's novel *Sula* and Mary Lamb and Sylvia Plath, to interpret her own life. She also uses her life—the time she felt so murderous toward her mother she nicked her with a carving knife, for example—to interpret and contextualize literature. She relates her rage at her mother to the character Sula's standing by, "interested," while her mother Hannah burned to death, and to Mary Lamb's murder of her mother with a knife and her subsequent significantly freer life in mental asylums where she no longer had to care for invalid parents and could devote more time to writing. The literary events Bernikow details are themselves lurid and provocative, but so are Bernikow's own personal narratives weaving in and out of her mixture of analyses and musings, twice-told tales and personal confession.

When, in "Sisters," Bernikow sets down that Louisa May Alcott's *Little Women* "ruined her life" because it presented an image of what she did not have, the reader senses her spontaneous praxis of the kind of the dialogic criticism, with its "drive 'to connect,'" both described and practiced by Patrocinio Schweickart in "Reading Ourselves: Toward a Feminist Theory of Reading." In fact, although Bernikow announces her allegiance to no modern critical method, her book attests to the confluence and interdependence of personal or interactive feminist criticism and other recent "isms" in what has been called the age of the reader.

Thus Sandra Gilbert wrote in 1979: "It is surely no coincidence that such an engaged and confessional way of thinking about literature was energized by the same era that brought us the so-called 'confessional' poets. . . . It is perhaps even more significant, moreover, that this political, autobiographical, and reader-centered criticism has evolved just in the years when we have moved, as M. H. Abrams recently noted . . . to an 'Age of the Reader'" ("Life Studies" 852–53). Gilbert had in mind such early works as Rich's *On Lies, Secrets, and Silence* and Griffin's *Woman and Nature,* writing which helped authorize the personal, relational criticism characteristic of *Among Women* and its still more recent peers—especially those quite analogous, reader-oriented texts, Rachel M. Brownstein's *Becoming a Heroine: Reading about Women in Novels* (1982) and Phyllis Rose's *Writing of Women* (1985).

It has always seemed to me that the best response to writing was a reflexive one: answer a poem with a poem, a journal with a journal.[18] And the best writing invites such a reflexive or imitative response. These writers make me want to respond in kind by speaking to both my life *and* my writing, which is my life. As Tess Gallagher rightly observes in her own literary-critical-autobiographical anthology, *A Concert of Tenses* (1986), "the poetic persona and the poet's own autobiography are more closely engaged than at any other time in poetic history" (72). Feminist poet-critics create a discourse of interaction versus abstraction and distance, inspiring not just by their message but their media, exhorting others to speak, not silence, their authentic voices. Just as Elbow calls for "more voices, more kinds of voices," and Leitch wants the genre of the journal article threatened, I'd like to see more of the open forms of feminism in the academy.

All practitioners of the creative amalgam, those who play with conventions of voice and tone, whether out of exuberance (a version of "jouissance"), a desire for subversion, a desire for a more authentic (re)creation of the self in language, or a Derridean conviction that the "domain and interplay of signification" extends "ad infinitum," share a nostalgia for origins even as they head away from them into play. (I particularly like to refer to the act and effect of women's cross-genre writing as "(re)creation." We *re-create* what we think we know about ourselves, our origins, and yet we recognize that each time we write, we *create* ourselves and our audience anew. Finally, writing for us is not so much allied with death or absence, as Foucault would have it, as with *recreation,* play—including joyous team efforts.)

Feminist writers create communion with other women as they persist in writing against their absence, silence, and invisibility. As Adrienne Rich quotes Susan Griffin to have said, "For a feminist, writing may be solitary but thinking is collective" (*LSS* 208). These writers' indebtedness to one another, and mine to them, demonstrates the relational and engendering power of that collective thinking and the resultant anomalous, inviting prose styles integrating and collapsing creative and critical discourses.

It may never be clear just how much of each practitioner's border crossing is the intentional or inevitable result of hybrid personal histories, a "drive to connect," the poststructuralist conviction of the interchangeability of discourses, research in rhetoric and composition, the tradition and example of women's "nontraditional" literature, the legacy of poetry, including so-called confessional poetry, or the formal experiments of previous poet-critics. What is clear, however, is that feminist poet-critics are increasingly celebrating multiple personal—and multiple textual—origins. Moreover, they are likely to foreground the image and process of recycling, of what Marge Piercy, in her poem "Out of the Rubbish," refers to as "workingclass making do." So it's no surprise that like other feminist critics, I welcome the sometime coalescence of other mixed literary-critical practices with American feminists' often political, autobiographical, reader-centered criticism. The next chapter focuses on recycling as another trope and explanation for recent feminist alchemy-amalgam-mosaics such as Piercy's *Parti-Colored Blocks for a Quilt,* Tess Gallagher's *Concert of Tenses,* Alice Walker's *In Search of Our Mothers' Gardens,* Susan Griffin's *Made from This Earth,* and Carol Ascher's, Louise DeSalvo's, and Sara Ruddick's *Between Women.*

FOUR

The Ecology of Alchemy, or, Recycling, Reclamation, Transformation in Marge Piercy, Tess Gallagher, Alice Walker, Susan Griffin, and in Carol Ascher's, Louise DeSalvo's, and Sara Ruddick's *Between Women*

The process of attending to and ignoring, dismembering and restoring forms another text that cannot confidently be pronounced either derivative or new.
Julia Kristeva, *Semiotike*

The mother tongue, spoken or written, expects an answer. It is conversation, a word the root of which means "turning together." The mother tongue is language not as mere communication, but as relation, relationship. It connects. . . . Its power is not in dividing but in binding.
Ursula LeGuin, quoted in Tompkins's "Me and My Shadow"

Theory—the seeing of patterns, showing the forest as well as the trees—theory can be a dew that rises from the earth and collects in the rain cloud and returns to earth over and over. But if it doesn't smell of the earth, it isn't good for the earth.
Adrienne Rich, "Notes toward a Politics of Location"

In a theoretical theatre that views multiplicity everywhere, a crowd is easily assembled, perhaps too easily in the case of my last chapter. So I read with amusement Gilles Deleuze and Felix Guattari's frank and funny comment at the beginning of *A Thousand Plateaus,* "The two of us wrote *Anti-Oedipus* together. Since each of us was several, there was already quite a crowd. Here we have made use of everything that came within range, what was closest as well as farthest away" (3). Deleuze and Guattari are quite right. The writer is already multiple, and her selves can easily be at cross-purposes with one another, creating a muddle of genres rather than a mosaic, a disordered collage rather than a coordinated colloquy. I was at cross-purposes with myself in chapter 3: I wanted to "read" Rushdie leisurely and yet needed to deliver on the promise in my title. I meant to attend not only to "episodes" but to published texts, both those of women poet-critics and those of several poststructuralist, reader-response, and composition theorists who signal the elision of criticism and literature in ways that echo feminist endeavors.

When I read *Anti-Oedipus,* I was very annoyed by Deleuze and Guattari's too quick, too crowded generation of acronyms and special terms. Deleuze and Guattari set my teeth on edge. I turned them into jokes and anagrams. When they referred to a "molar dog," I thought of "canines," a double entendre on dog and teeth. When they used BwO to designate the "Body-without-Organs," I couldn't help seeing BwO as an anagram of bow, as in bow-wow. I grew impatient. I couldn't reconcile molar dogs with the vegetable vocabulary of "rhizome" and later "arborescent culture." I wanted to know which author thought of which turn of phrase, which molecule of text. Where were *their* organs? Why this kind of organization, both textual and conceptual?

By contrast, I was relieved to read in *A Thousand Plateaus* the kind of metadiscourse I have come to attribute to feminist poet-critics, the kind that contextualizes a work and its composition for the reader. To make a distinction my elementary school teachers were fond of making in their efforts to teach politeness, I could now laugh *with* Deleuze and Guattari rather than *at* them. And I can also read myself in at least a couple of their textual gestures. As I write, I too am likely to "use everything . . . within range," including some of Deleuze and Guattari's words and practices. Julia Kristeva and other poststructuralists would theorize the impulse—which I earlier borrowed Marge Piercy's phrase to call "workingclass making do"—as being on some level every writer's method.

Clearly, in my own case this is so. I like to think, however, that despite its simply being ubiquitous, the impulse to recite, remake, recycle is for me—as it is for a welter of feminist poet-critics—both thrifty and generous. When I earlier quoted generously (as they say) from Tompkins's "Me and My Shadow," I was in fact demonstrating her own theory of generous (also generative) appreciation of others' words. Tompkins herself quotes extensively from both Susan Griffin and Ursula LeGuin. Then she comments, "Much of what I'm saying elaborates or circles around these quotations of LeGuin. I find that having released myself from the duty to say things I'm not interested in, in a language I resist, I feel free to entertain other people's voices. *Quoting them becomes a pleasure of appreciation* rather than the obligatory giving of credit, because when I write in a voice that is not struggling to be heard through the screen of forced language, *I no longer feel it is not I who am speaking, and so there is more room for what others have said"* (174; emphasis mine). Tompkins advocates an interactive as well as intertextual rhetoric in which the generous providing of space for others' words generates a chain of connections. As gracious host, she serves not to waylay us with the fabulous appointments of her mansion or with a sumptuous spread of food too beautiful to eat. Instead, she lets her friends become friends, gives up being queen bee, gives up a need for showy splendor, academic superiority, in favor of "turning together," conversation. I quoted Tompkins in the open way she quotes LeGuin and Griffin; suddenly Tompkins touches me "where I want to be touched," just as she thinks Griffin touches her readers. And I hope I touch you.

The thrifty, throw-nothing-away part of the impulse to borrow and quote is perhaps best demonstrated by what I term *intra-* or *inner-textuality,* the quoting or reworking of one's own old texts or tropes in newer texts. Here's an example.

I wrote a three-hundred-page autobiography the summer before I turned thirty. I wrote with at least two central motives, exorcising and explaining the personal pain I felt beset by that year, and finding a home for my orphaned poems. I proceeded chronologically except for certain "interchapters," and each chapter was interrupted or interleaved with poems; I found them berths as I described each of their "births" in time. I had a notion that I couldn't write new poems until I'd published or placed my fat packet of old ones somewhere first. I needed to claim and explain those voices before I could move on to others. (I'm not alone in regarding my poems as children, whether wayward or, worse, stillborn. Sylvia Plath and Anne Sexton have many poems expressly on the subject.)[1] But what I'm leisurely leading to is not a discussion of poems as children but of poems as patchwork, as "parti-colored blocks for a quilt," or as seed packets that feminist poet-critics such as Marge Piercy and Alice Walker feel impelled to sew or sow into a mostly prose quilt or garden. I hadn't wanted to waste or lay waste to my still-vivid (as in colorful as fabric, lively or alive as seedlings) poems. So, one of the characteristic features of many feminist poet-critics' border-crossing works is the incorporation of other or older voices (not just others' but their own) in generous and thrifty, often moving, ways.

Growing flowers or food from scratch, say from seeds, is an image both thrifty (as in saving money, especially when the seeds are not bought but retrieved from last year's harvest) and generous (we broadcast the seeds for better germination or share our bounty with others or spend generous amounts of time tending seedlings and weeding on our knees). A garden is even more the site of generosity, thrift, history, and community when one gardener transplants things growing in another's garden. To my garden, for example, I added my friend Juliet's irises, lavender, silver thyme, and columbine, and she took my lemon balm to hers. I could buy cut flowers from a florist or supermarket, but then I'd miss the simultaneously dirty and delightful detour through my own garden and my friends'.

Good gardeners and homesteaders use, appreciate, and conserve good tools and materials. In the United States in the 1990s, ecological conservation and a commitment to recycling materials such as aluminum, paper, glass, and plastic (to save the energy that would be used to produce aluminum, for example; to save the land and seascapes from acres of plastic waste; in short, to recover some of the money, time, technology, and space used in the making of the item in the first place) are equated with progressive politics. It is not usually considered politically conservative to conserve, to put up preserves and conserves from one's own garden.

"To Be of Use": Marge Piercy

In an interview she calls "Afterthoughts," Marge Piercy responds to Ira Wood's query, "Where did you come to love nature so much? How did you develop that interest?" by saying, "My mother who was a child of the slums, of extreme poverty, taught me to love natural beauty. She grew a lot of flowers in a tiny urban yard in Detroit. We had a lush backyard for the tinyness of it, for the extreme industrialization of the landscape" (*PCB* 325). In her poem "Out of the Rubbish," thrifty, generous, and historical acts such as the tending of plants and the saving of material(s) are echoed and brought back to life, to memory, when Piercy, sorting through her dead mother's things, finds

> a bottle-cap flower: the top
> from a ginger ale
> into which had been glued
> crystalline beads from a necklace
> surrounding a blue bauble.
> (*MMB* 11)

Just as in Rich's "Power," where the sight/site of "one bottle amber perfect" opens a space for contemplation, both for the rest of the poem and for a view of memory itself being, like the bottle, "a tonic / for living on this earth," Piercy's unearthing

of "this star-shaped posy / in the wreath of fluted / aluminum"
opens for her "a receding vista." This time, the view is of generic
"workingclass making do" and Piercy's personal, domestic past:

> A receding vista opens
> of workingclass making do:
> the dress that becomes
> a blouse that becomes
> a doll dress, potholders,
> rags to wash windows.
> Petunias in the tire.
> Remnants of old rugs
> laid down over the holes
> in rugs that had once
> been new when the rem-
> nants were first old.
>
> . . . .
>
> If we make curtains
> of the rose-bedecked table
> cloth, the stain won't show
> and it will be cheerful,
> cheerful. Paint the wall lime.
> Paint it turquoise, primrose.
>
> . . . .
>
> In the window, ceramic
> bunnies sprouted cactus.
> A burro offered fuchsia.
> In the hat, a wandering Jew.
> *That was your grandfather.*
> *He spoke nine languages.*
> (*MMB* 11–13)

By opening a vista, the flower represents more than thrift; it rep-
resents a familial flowering from roots both working class and
Jewish, a family that speaks the "language of flowers." The vista
also suggests the grown daughter's openness to the nobility as
well as pity of her mother's life, the pity and pain entering in the
stanza of remembered mother-daughter conversation:

> Don't you ever want to
> travel? *I did when I*
> *was younger. Now, what*
> *would be the point?*
> *Who would want to meet me?*
> *I'd be ashamed.*
> (*MMB* 13)

The flower represents the bud, and also blight, of possibility; it represents the pleasure, if not art, attainable (even) in a working-class idiom, and it represents too the guilt or shamed embarrassment that pleasure—or time taken from more pressing or traditional tasks—might signal,[2] at least for Piercy's mother:

> One night alone she sat
> at her kitchen table
> gluing baubles in a cap.
> When she finished,
> pleased, she hid it away
> where no one could see.
> (13).

Piercy both adopts and abridges her mother's aesthetic. (As Kristeva would say, her aesthetic "cannot confidently be pronounced either derivative or new"; it is both.) Out of a remnant, a piece of the past (the pieced nature of the past is underscored in the line breaking the word "remnants" into the pieces "rem-" and "nants"), a beaded flower patch, Piercy creates a whole if limited landscape, the braided rug, the patchwork quilt, the garden that is this poem. Piercy's mother's legacy to her is one of thrift and beauty, hard work and art. Piercy might have said, and certainly implies, precisely what Alice Walker writes in her essay "In Search of Our Mothers' Gardens": "Guided by my heritage of a love of beauty and a respect for strength—in search of my mother's garden, I found my own" (*MG* 243). In "Lunar Cycle," an essay, Piercy specifically identifies her mother and other women poets writing about their mothers as her inspirations. She states she had wanted to write a poem about her mother but lacked "the theoretical framework" until reading the writing of several Black women, "especially June Jordan's 'Getting Down to Get Over' and the many poems Audre Lorde has written about her mother." Piercy then adds, "I have a strong sense that my mother formed me as a poet and a strong sense of how first poverty, and then the iron sex roles of working-class life, had confined her, warped her: and yet the gifts she gave me were precious and radiant with energy" (*PCB* 76). Unlike her mother, however, Piercy does not hide away her constructions, even if they may be deemed (as Piercy's mother might have viewed her bottle-cap flower) impractically, even foolishly, sentimental—or at the least, not things of indisputable beauty.

In the poem, in fact, we are told that "it is not / as a thing of beauty" that the daughter carried off her mother's beadwork but as a memento or token leading to the "vista" on "workingclass making do," which is not merely an aesthetic and personal vision but one social, historical, and political. Both in her poems and in her literary criticism, Piercy is less insistent than many others on creating the beautiful or the "purely literary." In "An Interview with Peggy Friedmann and Ruthann Robson of *Kalliope,*" Piercy describes the kind of feminist criticism she is inclined to read (and write) as that with "a certain amount of sociological underpinnings or historical value" (*PCB* 138). Piercy values her mother's bottle-cap flower less as a work of art than as an expression of her mother's experience and eye. In "Shaping Our Choices," Piercy praises what she calls "all that amateur substratum in the arts," theorizing that "a society in which a whole lot of people sing is a society that really understands a great singer. . . . A society in which a great number of people write poems for each other—with perfect assurance that what they're doing is nice—is also the one in which people appreciate writing!" (*PCB* 39). She rebels against what she was taught as a child growing up in the fifties, that everything in art fit "somewhere in a vast hierarchy" ("Through the Cracks," *PCB* 115).

Piercy consistently explores and values constructive, survivalist work, from political protest to writing to handicrafts or home arts such as gardening and quilting, especially as they keep one in touch with one's familial history or the cycles of nature. As she tells it in "The Rose and the Eagle":

> Crimson roses and red causes,
> savoy cabbage and grand juries:
> both write poems through
> me. . . .
> (*TSW* 94)

In her brief biography at the back of *The Twelve-Spoked Wheel Flashing* (1978), the book from which these lines come, Piercy writes that she and her housemates grow all their own vegetables and a "fair amount" of fruit. She further notes that she tried to shape the book "as a growth ring, the record of a year." In a review, Diane Wakoski calls Piercy "one of the pioneers of twentieth-century earth poetry" (7). Piercy titled an early book of poems *To Be of Use* (1973), and she speaks repeatedly of the work involved in loving, making a community, gardening—calling a book of poems *Hard Loving* (1969), a novel *Braided Lives,* and a collection of nonfiction prose *Parti-Colored Blocks for a Quilt.* Like Rich, whom she quotes, Piercy believes "increasingly that only the willingness to share private and sometimes painful experiences can enable women to create a collective description of the world which will be truly ours" (Rich, quoted in Piercy, *PCB* 269). Her hope is to join with other women who "are working to make part of the same quilt to keep us from freezing to death in a world that grows harsher and bleaker—where male is the norm and the ideal human being is hard, violent and cold: a macho rock. Every woman who makes of her living something strong and good is sharing bread with us" (*PCB* 4).

The vocabulary of both quilting and gardening clearly crops up throughout Piercy's corpus and her commentary upon it. In "The First Salad of March," Piercy celebrates "lettuce / fresh as a tear" (*TSW* 38), then tells it, in "The Love of Lettuce,"

> You grow out of last year's
> composted dinner and you
> will end in my hot mouth
> (*TSW* 43).

Piercy is aware of food for mouth (and poems) being something both fresh and derivative. As poet and essayist Robert Pinsky says, "The instrument of poetry is the mouth." Moreover, Piercy's poems, like her vegetables, are worked by her own hands in conjunction with nature('s). And like her poems themselves and her "limping causes," planting—whether of edibles or not—both represents and demonstrates Piercy's ongoing hope and faith, as she says directly in "Seedlings in the Mail":

> Like mail order brides
> they are lacking in glamor.
> Drooping and frail and wispy,
> they are orphaned waifs of some green catastrophe
> from which only they have been blown to safety
> swaddled in a few wraiths of spagnum moss.
> Windbreaks, orchards, forests of the mind
> they huddled in the dirt
> smaller than our cats.
> The catalog said they would grow
> to stand ninety feet tall.
> I could plant them in the bathroom.
> I could grow them in window pots,
> twelve trees to an egg carton.
> I could dig four into the pockets of my jeans.
> I could wear some in my hair
> or my armpits.
> Ah, for people like us, followed
> by forwarding addresses and dossiers and limping causes
> it takes a crazy despairing faith
> full of teeth as a jack o-lantern
> to plant pines and fir and beech
> for somebody else's grandchildren,
> if there are any.
> (*COW* 147)

Here, as elsewhere, Piercy exposes a central theme much like the one Pinsky recently named as his own, which also carries with it a hint of gardening imagery: "a quality of courage or heart that lets one continue to live with relish, despite risk and misfortune in the world. One way to account for this is to go back to seek its *roots*" (emphasis mine). Piercy praises this quality in others when she praises Rich for believing that "thought is most useful, most authentic when *rooted* in our body," for writing a book [*Of Woman Born*] "*rooted* in the deeply, painfully personal" (*PCB* 271; emphasis mine). And Piercy practices what she praises.

Also in her interview "Afterthoughts," Piercy concedes that sometimes she'll "be aware of a poem which is also the same germination as the novel" and that she took her novel title *Braided Lives* from her poem "Looking at Quilts" (*PCB* 321). She says, "I write in organic verse which is the predominant poetic form of our time" (*PCB* 29): "The little poems of the day are simple, but sometimes in them comes a *seed,* a flash, that real word that summons real work" (*PCB* 327; emphasis mine). Or she'll get the originary words, image, or idea while reading poetry she then recycles, rewrites into a poem or essay. As she describes in her essay "Inviting the Muse," "It need not even be poetry. That quotation from Thoreau ['That afternoon the dream of the toads that rang through the elms by the Little River and affected the thoughts of men . . .'] that begins this essay instigated a poem called 'Toad Dreams.' I remember starting a poem in the middle of reading a *Natural History* magazine or the *Farmer's Almanac*" (*PCB* 8). Piercy's admitted tendency to reclaim and transform texts of others, texts of the past, reminds me again of Rich, who in "reading about Marie Curie" is led into writing a poem, "Power," woven of that reading, her reverie, and what else she sees before her ("a crumbling flank of earth").

Piercy's inspirations and imagistic borrowings clearly come not only from personal, feminist, and hippie history and experience, but from nineteenth-century American Transcendentalists, probably from Whitman as much as Thoreau. Whitman and

Piercy seek and admire the self-made; Whitman's "curling grass" and sensuality (*Leaves of Grass,* especially "Song of Myself") are echoed in Piercy's "pale green curly lust" over "oakleaf, buttercrunch, ruby, cos" lettuce and life (*TSW* 43); Whitman's "scent of these armpits finer than prayer" (1.525) is alchemized into Piercy's line about wearing seedlings in "my hair/or my armpits" ("Seedlings," *COW* 147). My point is not to catalog an exhaustive list of a poet's influences, but to show that Piercy not only transplants and coalesces many texts and voices in her work but suggests that fact in the imagery of growing things. Scholars often argue about what constituted Whitman's "long foreground" before he wrote *Leaves of Grass,* "ground" being the right image for one who wrote, "My tongue, every atom of my blood, formed from this soil" (1.6); part of Piercy's foreground, I figure, was her reading the words of Whitman and Thoreau so that she might absorb and transform them.[3] I make a pun, in the tradition of Thoreau: Piercy indeed received some seedlings in the mail/male, wind- or book-blown bits of language from men of letters. Of course, her roots also lie in her own mother's garden and with Rich, Jordan, Lorde, and still others.

Piercy's accessible, usually first-person, "lyric-narrative" poetic quickly orients her readers, makes them feel at home. Piercy demonstrates what Tess Gallagher describes as the "cozy use of ego in American poetry in which the 'I' seems often in exact coincidence with the poet in divulging family secrets" (*Concert of Tenses* 53). I don't agree with Gallagher, however, that such writing produces "in some poets a state of near psychic bankruptcy," especially because Piercy's "I" (and eye) seem expansive, what with her commitment to a "strong sense of responsibility" toward others. Piercy's work does tally with Gallagher's other astute observation, however, that the lyric poem is often so entirely dependent on narrative and anecdotal strategies that the distinction between the narrative and the lyric has been greatly blurred: "What we really have now in contemporary poetry is a hybrid of two forms, narrative and lyric . . . we now have a term like the lyric-narrative to describe the most prevalent contemporary development of these forms" (72). The patchwork or blurring or doubling of genres is thus early at work in Piercy's poems as well as present in her quilted, hybrid critical prose. Moreover, the way in which Piercy turns art conventionally considered "low" (beads glued in a bottle cap) into the subject or seed of an art conventionally thought "high(er)" (poetry) is echoed or recycled in a prose style that mixes not only poetry with prose (traditionally considered low relative to poetry) but anecdote and conversation with eloquence, political oratory, and at times, extended poetic conceit. Piercy even makes the conversational form of the interview serve as several of the "particolored blocks" that form her quilt of a book, with each block or interview itself a compendium of autobiography and literary theory, jokes and quotes.

The last essay of Piercy's *Parti-Colored Blocks for a Quilt,* "Margaret Atwood: Beyond Victimhood," contains the passage joining growing and quilting I cite in a previous chapter (and cannot resist recycling here). In this essay, Piercy figures women's culture, to which Atwood's works contribute, as both a "*growing* body" and a "great *quilt* for which we are each stitching our own particolored blocks out of old petticoats, skirts, coats, bedsheets, blood, and berry juice" (299; emphasis mine); she transforms and interweaves garden bounty (berries) and bodily fluids (blood) imagistically into a quilt, and both grow into (and in) a quilt of words.

Throughout her writing, including poetry, prose, and interviews, Piercy fulfills her own sense of what feminism involves: "a strong sense of history, a strong sense of ourselves in nature, in natural cycles, and a strong sense of responsibility to each other when we need aid" ("Shaping Our Choices," *PCB* 45). Aware that some of her readers love her poems "about zucchini and lettuce and tomatoes, and simply skip or tune out the poems about an old working-class woman lying in a nursing home or about nuclear power," and that others love the poems "they call feminist or political," but ask why she writes "about blue heron and oak trees," Piercy confesses that for her "it is all one vision" (22). "For Shoshana Rihn—Pat Swinton" makes clear how for Piercy a feminist re-vision of history is allied with nature. Women's history (and the poetry that incorporates it) is seen as organic, a great, green, growing body:

> Beyond official history of texts,
> of bronze generals,
> a history flows of rivers and amoebas,
> of the first creeping thing
> that shuddered onto the land,
> a history of the woman who
> tamed corn, a history
> of learning and losing, a history
> of making good and being had,
> of some great green organism
> gasping to be free . . .
> (*COW* 217)

For the other feminist poet-critics discussed in this chapter, the homespun, the homestead, and nature similarly conspire to form fertile ground for their communal feminist poetics and politics, their cross-genre work. As Wakoski insists in her assessment of Piercy: "Perhaps one of the greatest contributions twentieth-century American women make to poetry is to refuse to let aestheticians and poets forget the body. The earth body, the goddess body, the seasons and cycles, the agrarian root which we must still have even in urban or post-urban culture" (7).

"Moss-light" and Memory: Tess Gallagher

Tess Gallagher herself practices a genre-blurring akin to the lyric-narrative style she describes in her book of creative criticism, *A Concert of Tenses: Essays on Poetry* (1986). Writing in the same University of Michigan series that earlier published Piercy's cross-genre *Parti-Colored Blocks for a Quilt,* Gallagher both contextualizes and rewrites her poetry, either in prose or in a prose preamble, recycling her own poems, the stories behind them, and others' writings to create the "concert of tenses" of her title.

Gallagher creates a collaborative (and musical) pastiche of past and present in which she allows the older voices of teachers, other poets, family, and self to speak together. In her first essay, "My Father's Love Letters," Gallagher inventories her influences as a writer. They include the rain of her birthplace, the Pacific Northwest—"the climate of her psyche" (2), a climate she demonstrates by the immediate inclusion, on pages 2 and 3, of a poem about it. "Sudden Journey" hints at a fertile compositional aesthetic:

> Maybe I'm seven in the open field—
> the straw-grass so high
> only the top of my head makes a curve
> of brown in the yellow. Rain then.
> First a little. A few drops on my
> wrist, the right wrist. More rain.
> My shoulders, my chin. Until I'm looking up
> to let my eyes take the bliss.
> I open my face. Let the teeth show. I
> pull my shirt down past the collar bones.
> I'm still a boy under my breast spots.
> I can drink anywhere. The rain. My
> skin shattering. Up suddenly, needing
> to gulp turning with my tongue, my arms out
> running, running in the hard, cold plenitude
> of all those who reach earth by falling.

She continues, in prose now: "Growing up there, I thought the moss-light that lived with us lived everywhere. . . . I always went outside with my eyes wide, no need to shield them from sun bursts or the steady assault of skies I was to know later in El Paso or Tucson. The colors of green and gray are what bind me to the will to write poems." The rain is generative. It has inspired this poem which recurs in a prose essay. (We might even say it's recycled in this poem and in all of Gallagher's work it inspires.) It opens the eyes, the face, "shatters" the skin, letting us into Gallagher's life and psyche; its "plenitude" makes for plenty. Gallagher here also echoes Gerard Manley Hopkins's recognition of the literally and spiritually generative status of rain; in "Thou are Indeed Just, Lord," he pleads, "O thou lord of life, send my roots rain."

In the prose passage following "Sudden Journey," Gallagher absorbs and transforms northwesterner Theodore Roethke's line "moss, wound with the last light" from his "Elegy for Jane." Moreover, Gallagher's reliance on northwest light and imagery as well as on Roethke comes up again in "An Interview with Rachel Berghash" and "Last Class with Roethke," among other places in *A Concert of Tenses,* suggesting a textual cycle to go with the water cycle productive of moss and subdued light. In her interview with Jeanie Thompson, for example, Gallagher says most directly, "Roethke was an early teacher . . . I got a love of Yeats from him that has been my strongest influence in a constant way" (29). In "My Father's Love Letters," we begin to see that Gallagher shares with Roethke not only a language and landscape, but, at least occasionally, the elegiac mode: "I think partings have often informed my poems with a backward longing" (19). She corroborates this notion in "The Poem as a Reservoir of Grief," an essay whose title patches together the rain, water, and tears alluded to in both "My Father's Love Letters" and Roethke's "Elegy for Jane"; there she writes, "poems have long been a place where one could count on being allowed to feel in a bodily sense our connection to loss" (103).

Gallagher continues describing her influences, confiding, "Along with rain and a subdued quality of light, I have needed the nearness of water" (3), and later, "trees have always been an important support to the solitude I connect with the writing of poetry." In a memory cycle akin to the water cycle, she moves, then, from rain to her childhood home in Port Townsend, Washington, overlooking eighteen miles of water, to living with her parents, her father's drinking, to memories of logging with her parents, and the love letters her father had sent to her mother. Inevitably, she sees her protofeminist mother ("whatever the rest of the world said about women, the woman my mother was stood equal to any man around and maybe one better") and her father as important influences. Together they establish the warp and woof of Gallagher's repeated textual images: water, drink, poems as love letters and (thus) vignettes of the past, and trees—in all their incarnations, as beauty and scenery, logs for firewood or for the logging mill, logs to become pulp or paper. Gallagher reproduces in full her poem "Black Money" on page 9, telling us this was the first poem that "reached" her father, its central image "taken from the way shoveling sulfur at the pulp mills had turned his money black." Both the reference to black money and the experience of family logging, not to mention feminism and the power of "moss-light" crop up elsewhere in *A Concert of Tenses*, attesting to Gallagher's simultaneous compositional thrift and generous dwelling on family and self-generation (see again, for example, the interviews with Thompson and Berghash).

The rest of "My Father's Love Letters" travels around the country of (and with) her poems, to Missouri, where Gallagher's mother was born and her uncle much later murdered, to Vietnam, where her first husband flew "fly missions" in the war, to Ireland and Europe, where Gallagher lived at that time. Gallagher remembers traveling to Missouri to meet her parents for the murder trial after her mother proved the uncle's death was a homicide, the killers having been found. Gallagher reproduces here her poem "Two Stories," dedicated "to the author of a story taken from the death of my uncle." "Two Stories" (re)tells the story of her uncle's murder as well as illustrates the recycling aesthetic I find at work in Gallagher, Piercy, Walker, and others:

> Now there is the story of me
> reading your story and the one
> of you saying it.
> (17)

She thus demonstrates and describes how for her poems are acts of reclamation: "After my youngest brother's death when I was twenty, I began to recognize the ability of poetry to extend the lives of those not present except as memory" (13); "I began to see poems as a way of settling scores with the self" (18).

Gallagher ultimately cycles back to the love letters in the essay's title: "I'm trying to understand why I keep remembering my father's love letters as having an importance to my own writing" (23). The connection finally becomes clearer, to both

Gallagher and her readers, whom Gallagher has led organically through her writing and thinking processes. In the best new feminist poet-critic tradition, Gallagher refuses to deny her personal history or the process by which she comes to know what she knows or believe what she believes (to paraphrase a description about feminist essays I give early in chapter 1). She tells us, "I think of my father's love letters being perused by the members of the [World War II] draft board. They become convinced that the courtship is authentic. They decide not to draft him in the war. As a result of his having written love letters, he does not go to his death and my birth takes place" (23). And the letters, now long since given to a draft board or burned, are revived, phoenixlike (or recycled, reclaimed), in Gallagher's own (literary) letters, as it were:

> I think of my father's love letters burning, of how they might never have come into their true importance had I not returned to them here in my own writing . . . they did not truly exist until this writing [or even this re-citing], even for my parents, who wrote and received them.[4]
>
> My father's love letters are the sign of a long courtship and I pay homage to that, the idea of writing as proof of the courtship—the same blind, persistent hopefulness that carries me again and again into poems. (23)

In an essay titled "Again" (apt given my focus as well as Gallagher's on recycling), Gallagher revises or rewrites Pound's precept "make it new" by saying (and demonstrating), "the poet must supplement Pound's dictum . . . with an acknowledgement that the reader and listener may also need to 'hear it old'" (69). She goes on:

> It is now the intimacy of voice, used as a poetic strategy, which establishes the hear-it-old requirement of the ancient narrative impulse—even though at first this intimacy might seem to accomplish exactly the opposite in making things feel all-too-much invested in the present moment. That is, hearing something told as-if-in-confidence establishes a context of "I'm only telling this to you." . . .
>
> We have what amounts to an instant history and mythmaking. . . . [It enables] the poet to preserve the sense of value, of

handed-downess, of treasuring what is told. The convention of intimacy, in this instance, serves as a kind of telescopic lens through which the poet's emotional experience is actually magnified and brought closer to the reader. . . . In this way, the tradition of hearing-it-old continues under different terms even as we hear it newly. (71)

Gallagher's aesthetic comes patched together from oral narrative tradition, Pound, her parents, and the landscapes and poets of the Pacific Northwest.

"My Mama's Generation": Alice Walker

The socially constructed virtues of women, the result of their long subordination, have redeeming qualities for all human beings. Women's capacities are to nurture, to affiliate with others, to work collectively.

Hester Eisenstein, *Contemporary Feminist Thought*

Like Piercy, Alice Walker not only weaves the image of her mother's garden into her work but self-consciously borrows and celebrates her mother's ability to make do, make beautiful, with whatever she has available. In the title essay of her creative-critical amalgam, *In Search of Our Mothers' Gardens,* Walker speaks of the creativity of the black woman having been kept alive in nonliterary forms in an America where "it was a punishable crime for a black person to read or write" (234). She rescues or reclaims eighteenth-century black American poet Phillis Wheatley, who, though she did actually write, has too often been deemed "fool" or traitor on account of her lily-white descriptions, as of a Goddess fair with golden hair. Cross-pollinating her essay with references to black artists Jean Toomer, Okot p'Bitek, and her own mother, along with Wheatley, Walker writes: "But at last, Phillis, we understand. . . . We know now that you were not an idiot or a traitor; only a sickly little black girl, snatched from your home and country and made a slave. . . . It is not so much what you sang, as that you kept alive, in so many of our ancestors, *the notion of a song*" (237).

Walker's own mother's creativity, she recalls, like that of many other black mothers' and grandmothers', was expressed (as well as muzzled) in her garden, in the vegetables and fruits she grew and canned, and in the clothes, towels, sheets, and quilts she made. "And so our mothers and grandmothers have, more often than not anonymously, handed on the creative spark, the seed of the flower they themselves never hoped to see: or like a sealed letter they could not plainly read" (240). Walker sees that "so many of the stories that I write, that we all write, are my mother's stories" (an observation obviously borne out in Piercy and Gallagher's work as well as Walker's). As Walker's mother adorned her prosaic lot, Walker adorns with her mother's image(s) the prose that in the U.S. in this century it is legal for her to write: "My mother adorned with flowers whatever shabby house we were forced to live in. And not just your typical straggly country stand of zinnias, either. . . . Because of her creativity with flowers, even my memories of poverty are seen through a screen of blooms—sunflowers, petunias, roses, dahlias, forsythia. . . . A garden so brilliant with colors, so original in its design, so magnificent with life and creativity, that to this day people drive by our house in Georgia . . . and ask to stand or walk among my mother's art" (241).

Walker's essay as a whole (indeed, her entire corpus) is a tribute to the art that is her mother's gift, her mother's legacy of "possibilities—and the will to grasp them," yet Walker caps off the tribute with a poem she calls "not enough, but . . . something, for the woman who literally covered the holes in our walls with sunflowers":

> They were women then
> My mama's generation . . .
> How they knew what we
> *Must* know
> Without knowing a page
> Of it
> Themselves.
> (242)

This cross-genre, meandering essay (moving in a kind of natural sauntering akin to Piercy's and Gallagher's, not to mention Thoreau's) concludes with the sentiment I suggest above is also Piercy's and to some extent Gallagher's as well (though Gallagher seeks her father's strength as well as her mother's and, because they were so readily available to her, the lyric lines of loss from male predecessors Yeats and Roethke):

> Guided by [my mother's] heritage of a love of beauty and a respect for strength—in search of my mother's garden, I found my own.
>
> And perhaps in Africa over two hundred years ago, there was just such a mother; perhaps she painted vivid and daring decorations . . . ; perhaps she sang. . . . Perhaps she herself was a poet—though only her daughter's name is signed to the poems we know.
>
> Perhaps Phillis Wheatley's mother was also an artist.
>
> Perhaps in more than Phillis Wheatley's biological life is her mother's signature made clear (Walker 243).

Other texts of Walker's "enable the poet to preserve the sense . . . of handed-downess, of treasuring what is told," to borrow Gallagher's terms, so that in more than Alice Walker's biological life are her mother's and teachers' and heroines' signatures—and blooms—made clear. Titling a collection of poems *Revolutionary Petunias,* for example, allows Walker to resurrect the petunias of her mother's garden, to tie beauty and art to politics, Walker's background ("seen through a screen of blooms") to her present linguistic forays. Walker says of Sammy Lou, the central figure in the poem "Revolutionary Petunias":

> Even on her way to the electric chair, [Sammy Lou] reminds her children to water [the flowers]. This is crucial for I have heard it said that whenever you hear a black person talking about the beauties of nature, that person is . . . a Negro. This is meant as a put-down, and it is. . . . in fact, it covers just about everybody's mama. Sammy Lou, of course, is so "incorrect" she does not even know how ridiculous she is for loving to see flowers blooming around her unbearably ugly gray house. To be "correct" she should consider it her duty to let ugliness reign . . . [Sammy Lou] is part of an ongoing revolution. (266–67)

Walker adds that another reason she named the poem "Revolutionary Petunias" is simply that she likes raising petunias: "You just put them in any kind of soil and they bloom their heads off—exactly, it seemed to me, like black people tend to do" (267–68). Then she tells the story of her mother once insisting her husband stop their wagon so she could get a petunia she saw blooming outside a deserted house. That petunia (Walker, like her mother, insists), unlike modern varieties, bloomed year after year, wherever the family settled. Walker asserts that in a way her whole volume is a celebration of people who "are all shouting Stop! I want to go get that petunia!" They stand for resistance, for not letting "the bloom they are after wither in the winter of self-contempt" (268–69).

Walker writes for and out of a community of others, recognizing the resonance for her or Marilou Awiakta's poem "Motheroot," the epigraph to "In Search of Our Mothers' Gardens":

> Creation often
> needs two hearts
> one to root
> and one to flower
> One to sustain
> in time of drouth
> and hold fast
> against winds of pain
> the fragile bloom
> that in the glory
> of its hour
> affirms a heart
> unsung, unseen.
> (231)

As Jean Barker-Nunn has asserted about the work of Maxine Hong Kingston and Kim Chernin, Walker too sees that "individual lives have very little meaning outside of the context of history and family" (57–58); in setting out to tell her own story, she too finds herself telling her mother's, discovers she needs one to tell the other (Barker–Nunn 58). Creation calls for collaboration. Thus, Barker-Nunn, writing about those other feminist texts, concludes, "it is within the circle, the web of connections that meaning is ultimately found" (60). Walker, like Piercy and Gallagher, tends to pattern both her life and her art in terms of the networks Carol Gilligan and others theorize that women tend toward (see Barker-Nunn 60). These poet-critics write out of and make a web of connections among mothers and sisters, literary history and autobiography, poetry and criticism. They find creative germination in the recycling, reworking, reclaiming of others' words and work.

In her talk at the 1972 Sarah Lawrence College convocation (collected in *In Search of Our Mothers' Gardens*), Walker speaks of both beautiful and deadly blooms: "No person is your friend (or kin) who demands your silence, or denies your right to grow and be perceived as fully blossomed as you were intended. . . . Ignorance, arrogance, and racism have bloomed as Superior Knowledge in all too many universities" (36). She makes a garland of the wonderful "women who were generally abused when they lived and wrote, or were laughed at and belittled, or were simply forgotten" (34)—Mrs. Winston Hudson, Lucy Terry, and the women she resurrects elsewhere as her literary heroines, Wheatley and Zora Neale Hurston (see "Looking for Zora" and "Zora Neale Hurston: A Cautionary Tale and a Partisan View"). She refuses "to be entirely pessimistic about Hurston et al. They did commendable and often brilliant work under distressing conditions. They did live full, useful lives." Their literary power no longer lies hidden or dormant; today, "their works are being read with gratitude by younger generations" (35).

Walker follows the first catalog with one of her former and inspiring teachers at Sarah Lawrence: Helen Merrell Lynd, Muriel Rukeyser (who helped her to publish her poems in the first place), and Jane Cooper. She loops them and the rest of the essay together with imagery of nurturing and generation: "These women were Sarah Lawrence's gift to me. And when I think of them, I understand that each woman is capable of truly bringing another into the world. This we must all do for each other" (39). Carrying on this (re)generative legacy, Walker ends with "a gift of two poems," both from *Revolutionary Petunias*. The last poem, "Reassurance," reassures by grafting onto the images of past generations the notion of self-generation:

and in the hourly *making*
of myself
no thought of Time
to force
to squeeze
the space
I *grow* into.
(*MG* 41; emphasis mine)

Walker's job, as daughter, mother, and artist, is to keep a hold on the past as she moves into the future. In "Zora Neale Hurston: A Cautionary Tale and a Partisan View," she insists: *"We are a people. A people do not throw their geniuses away.* And if they are thrown away, it is our duty *as artists and as witnesses for the future* to collect them again for the sake of our children, and, if necessary, bone by bone" (92).[5] Both practical and deeply reverential, Walker does not want her people to throw away, waste, or consume the past but to collect it, skeletally if necessary, or more like a handed-down quilt, in which each piece of patchwork is itself a hand-me-down, preserving a bit of the past.

The quilt image is central in Walker's short story "Everyday Use" from her collection *In Love and Trouble.* It fits with what we already know Walker values—the usefulness as well as beauty of all her mother's domestic arts, for example, or the fact that Hurston led a "useful" life as well as or because of her literary one. Walker likes arts that are useful, whether for radical politics or everyday life, and she values an intergenerational or communal appreciation of domestic arts over that of an alienated or misinformed public. In "Everyday Use," Walker opposes a worldly daughter Dee/Wangero to the homebound Maggie, a contrast most apparent in the way each woman is inclined to treat not only her mother and homestead but her aunt's and grandmother's quilt.

"Everyday Use" is narrated by the mother of the two women, who early on reveals that Maggie was burned in the fire of their first house and has walked with "chin on chest, eyes on ground, feet in a shuffle, ever since." Dee, who after going away to school, settled in another place and is coming home to visit, "is lighter than Maggie, with nicer hair and a fuller figure" (49). With an attitude simultaneously disapproving and impressed, the mother-narrator describes Dee repeatedly in terms of "style"—"she had a style of her own: and she knew what style was"—and makes several references to the fact that Dee "forced words" on her family and read to her few childhood friends (50). Both of these attributes are seen somehow to render Dee, who has never had much time to give to her mother and sister, insensitive to the needs and pleasures of her country family. Soon Dee arrives with a man she introduces as Asalamalakim, introducing herself by her new name Wangero, explaining, "I couldn't bear it any longer being named after people who oppress me" (53). The two, full of themselves as liberated Afro-Americans in their Afro hair styles and dashikis, refuse to take to heart the mother's reminder that Dee was named after her aunt, who was named after Dee's grandmother and a woman before her. It is from this grandmother and aunt that Maggie, not Dee/Wangero, learned to quilt, though Dee has come demanding the quilts along with the old hand-carved top to the butter churn.

These art objects hold and encode family history; the quilts, for example, contain "scraps of dresses Grandma Dee had worn fifty or more years ago," "bits and pieces of Grandpa Jarrell's Paisley shirts," and "one teeny faded blue piece . . . that was from Great Grandpa Ezra's uniform that he wore in the Civil War" (56). But these heirlooms (or others like them) are also functional, not only in their intention, but in their present, everyday use at the narrator and Maggie's homestead. Dee wants the top of the butter churn as a centerpiece for a table; she wants to hang up the quilts for display, and she insists on taking Polaroid after Polaroid of her family standing in front of the ramshackle house the mother "deliberately turn[s] [her] back on" (51). Dee seems to have internalized a version of what Caren Kaplan terms theoretical tourism, a critical vacation, a poetics of the exotic (191). Dee has come inventorying and appropriating her family's outsiderhood; she makes them—and herself—*other*wise than they were.

Of the younger Dee, the mother had declared, "Dee wants nice things. . . . She was determined to stare down any disaster in her efforts" (50). Apparently, many years later, Dee/Wangero still "stares down" but doesn't see her family's past disasters or present reality. She ignores her mother's comment that the two oldest quilts have already been promised to Maggie, "for when she marries John Thomas" (57). But just when ever-acquiescent Maggie finishes saying, "She can have them, Mama . . . I can 'member Grandma Dee without the quilts," "something hit [the mother] in the top of [her] head and ran down to the soles of [her] feet": she has an epiphany. So the mother hands the quilts back to Maggie, despite Dee/Wangero's loud protest that Maggie doesn't understand her heritage, and her condescending, departing injunction, "You ought to try to make something of yourself, too, Maggie. It's really a new day for us" (58–59).

While the story is understated (or certainly much more so than Walker's essays), it is clear Walker is on the side of the mother and Maggie, and that Maggie has already made something "of herself," by herself—quilts, and a life with both her mother and the man she is about to marry. Or having confirmed her connection with the quilts, her mother, aunt, and grandmother, Maggie now "makes something of herself" out of something of them, and she can smile "a real smile, not scared" (59). She can *be* herself (unlike Dee/Wangero, whose self-making is viewed as artificial and contrived, remote from the threads and roots of her familial past). Maggie and her mother then sit "there just enjoying," connected and content.

Both Walker and Piercy see the quilts of yesterday as models and inspiration for writing today, and for communal and creative connections among women; quilts look back to and call forth collaboration. Viewed alongside "In Search of Our Mothers' Gardens," the quilt that begins as an emblem of family history for Walker widens (like Walker's mother's garden) into an emblem of creativity for an extended family of female artists. It thus works well as material for border-crossing work and as a matrix for new associations and stories, new connections.

In "Me and My Essay: A Proposal for a New Academic

Essay Written in My Own Voice," Cheryl B. Torsney suggests that a literary criticism written in her own voice "might look more like a quilt, pieced together, than like what we recognize as an academic article that 'pretends,' as William Gass writes, 'that everything is clear, that its argument is unassailable, that there are no soggy patches, no illicit interferences, no illegitimate connections'" (1–2). Later, she says, "in the kind of criticism I want to write, I want to talk openly about . . . personal circumstances," so she writes about reading and teaching Walker's story in the context of her visits to Mississippi State Penitentiary, where, as part of research she was doing on quilting as a metaphor in women's writing, she interviewed a female inmate who had pieced a quilt for a prison-hospital psychologist who knew Torsney's husband.

Narrative takes over for Torsney just as it did for the quilter, Lucille Sojourner, who "pieces together" her story for her hearer. Sojourner quilted first for a woman who wanted warmth from the prison cold; Lucille herself needed the money for her family outside and to buy food at the canteen, since the prison food was not only unpalatable but likely to cause food poisoning. Then she was commissioned by people outside who paid her well and still sold her quilts at a profit themselves. Our outside narrator, Torsney, begins to wonder, was she wrong somehow to commission a quilt herself? Was she acting like Dee, whom Torsney describes as "the flashy sister who is trying to 'preserve' her past in the sterile, academic hanging out of the family linen as though it were a formal blazon" (9)?

Torsney provides no easy answer as she moves from Dee and Lucille to a call for evocative writing that gives the readers of critical essays choices: "I want to leave my name and address at the end of the essay and encourage my readers to respond with their own experiences of a text so that they will enrich my context, allow me to stitch their reading histories into my critical texts of the narrative" (10). Like Gallagher, who in her poem "Two Stories" layers or recycles stories, or Tompkins, who quotes others in a gesture of appreciation I then emulate, reappropriate, Torsney and I are inclined to respond in kind, to partake of the same quilting tradition that so enriches the context and voice(s) of literary criticism. In just this spirit, Torsney based her title, "Me and My Essay," on Tompkins's "Me and My Shadow."

More and more, to write in one's own voice means writing in and with and directly to others' voices. Thus Piercy, Gallagher, Griffin (discussed below), and others consider interviews to be creative literary commentary. The interview, like the personally invested critical essay, may make reader and writer ever more conscious of the writer's voice, heard perhaps most clearly in the context of other voices, something Susan Griffin's polyvocal works repeatedly convey.

Modeled on This Earth: Susan Griffin

This earth holds a vast wisdom and a capacity to heal that
we are only beginning to comprehend. We are made from
this earth. This is my hope.
Introduction, *Made from This Earth*

As I've suggested in other chapters, poet-critic Susan Griffin is often concerned with defying patriarchy's injunction that women be silent or subscribe to dualities such as the separation of mind from body, emotions from logic. Like Piercy, Walker, and Gallagher, Griffin is concerned with keeping in touch with natural cycles and with herself as a woman. Her 1982 anthology *Made from This Earth* in large part defies generic classification, weaving (or composting) together as it does interviews, diary entries, essays, reviews, and sections from her books of poetry and prose, which themselves weave in myths, fables, epigraphs, and aesthetic manifesto. In several different places, Griffin refers to finding her voice in the context of other voices.

In a headnote to her "Interviews on Abortion," Griffin writes, "In 1969 and 1970, I recorded several interviews with women who had had abortions. I did not pretend to be an objective interviewer. I had had an illegal abortion myself, and I conducted these recordings like conversations" (21). Although she adds that in this recycled version of the interviews, she edited out some of her responses, the headnote supplements her voice asking the questions; the portrait painter is still in the painting (to borrow a notion from the introduction to *Between Women,* the final text to be discussed in this chapter).

The women who speak of the horrors of back-alley abortions, of doctors misdiagnosing them or raping them before operating, of mothers who come through with the abortion money in a clinch, help author-ize Griffin's "entrance into the feminist," her rage, the personal texture of all her writing. She responds as much as inquires and prompts: "You're lucky that she was there to help you." When a woman identified as K. L. thinks about the question of whether she wanted to get pregnant, Griffin responds sympathetically, offering up her own theory and personal experience. K. L. says: "I think it's not untypical for young women . . . that the only thing that convinces you that you are real is some sort of somatic reality . . . and that if you are not convinced of your body's existence, your existence, you are also not convinced of the body's capacity to conceive. I didn't think it could happen to me." Then Griffin responds: "I think such a feeling may be in part a result of a pristine silence our society cultivates on the subject of sex outside marriage. . . . When I was sixteen, you had to know the right gynecologist" (27). The give-and-take of the conversations embodies the very result Griffin claims she hoped for in publishing the interviews: "The book I was compiling was to encourage women to speak out against the inhumane treatment they have suffered" (21).

In her poem "A Woman Defending Herself Examines Her Own Character Witness" (275), Griffin uses an interview format somewhat reminiscent of Yeats or Marvell poems similarly arranged,[6] though her own poem is set as courtroom drama. Moreover, Griffin is concerned with what it means to be consciously a woman. The character witness answers the question "Who am I?" with "You are a woman." She explains, in response to still more questions, that she came to know the questioner through her own "pain and suffering," through becoming self-conscious, a process that took a long time because of the lies she was told. Although conscious of the fact that "lies were told" and "lies are still told" about women, the witness says she finally "stopped hearing lies" when her "own feelings became too loud." As the witness dramatizes in the poem by a sustained speech listing the attributes of the questioner, which are also those of the witness-with-raised-consciousness, she "could not silence [her] own feelings any longer": "You are a woman who has had enough. / You are a woman clear in your rage. / And they are afraid of you." She speaks on and on. And then, despite the questioner's retort that "if you go on with this line you will be instructed to remain silent" (to which the witness replies, "And that is what they require of us"), the witness and the questioning self have both spoken in a way that cannot be "stricken from the record," though the questioner says the long speech should be. The poem represents a successful negotiation of the voices of prohibition; the writer/self testifies that she will not permit even the (internalized) voice of repression to silence her own feelings any longer. The record of a "woman who is angry," "who speaks too loudly," and so on, remains, appearing not only in *Made from This Earth* but earlier in *Like the Iris of an Eye*, Griffin's 1976 collection of poems.

In the introduction to *Made from This Earth*, Griffin confesses she likewise needed two voices to write *Woman and Nature: The Roaring Inside Her* (1978), "one a parody of the scientific voice in which I answered my own fear of authority by making fun of the disembodied, seemingly 'objective' voice of authority. The other voice would be the embodied, feeling voice of woman and nature. Now I had two characters and a drama. The voice of authority—a male and patriarchal voice— attempted over and over again to dominate the female voice of the body, of forests, of wind, of mountains, of horses, cows, of the earth" (16).

Griffin claims this kind of juxtaposition made her able to see, for example, that what "motivates rape also motivates the destruction of ecological balance: the desire to dominate nature, to be in control" (17). Not only did she now also see that "the derogatory way in which men see women was a mirror of culture's derogatory view of matter" (17), but she could now think of her writing, and write of her thinking, as in-process, organic,

transformative, in keeping with her frequent subject, "the deli-
cate cycles which keep the soil alive" ("Transformations," *MFE*
220). In this way, Griffin's composing style reminds me of what
I've called the naturally meandering methods of Walker, Piercy,
and Gallagher, not to mention Rich. (See my discussion in chap-
ter 2 of Rich's associatively drifting prose style echoing her
acknowledged drifting into closer association with Jews and
Judaism. There, for Rich, it was *indistinct knowing;* here, for
Griffin, it is what might be termed *organic knowing* or discover-
ing.)

In talking further about *Women and Nature* in "Thoughts
on Writing: A Diary," Griffin speaks of how she wanted a kind of
symmetry and repetition built into the structure and how, al-
though at first they began to occur through conscious effort,
they continued to occur "unbidden," in a natural emulation of
"the patterns of the universe that it envisioned" (*MFE* 232). She
cites a "meditation that is also an old Shamanistic practice" in
which one becomes that on which one concentrates—animal,
shell, tree, and so on. "As one writes *about* a phenomenon, one's
words begin to mimic that phenomenon, to become that which
they describe" (232). Griffin, like Piercy, Walker, and Gallagher,
takes up the organically (or "intuitively"; 132) constructed for
both form and content. But as I have shown in chapter 2, Griffin
also shares with Piercy and Walker a reverence for and recourse
to the homespun, as when she speaks of women's words weav-
ing together and bringing women both toward one another "and
outward, expanding the limits of the possible" (220). Though
Griffin does not speak like these others of her writing self as
descending from a gardening, logging, or quilting mother, she
does identify her writing and vocal self with her (feminist)
sisters: "The discovery of my own voice as a writer occurred
simultaneously with my entrance into the feminist," she insists
(187).

When I view these authors' intratextual books together, I see
that I alternately recognize them as organic wholes and as col-
lections, with each selection a distinct piece of the quilt that is
the book (or, at times, that is the composite book of the work of

all such writers). It strikes me that an anthology or collection provides a reinforcing context for writings that are themselves mini-anthologies, collections of different genres and voices, compendia of the new and derivative. (The anthology stitches together materials that have been basted together to form blocks, but are not yet further connected. It also quilts them to a backing.) Like the interview, the anthology expresses in a kind of visual onomatopoeia the reliance on the collective espoused or thematized in several individual selections. The anthologies of Piercy, Gallagher, Walker, and Griffin enact what they announce, embody a performative or double-density rhetoric. The collections may not be symmetrical—that is, each selection does not precisely echo, in small, the structure of the whole—but the spirit of the whole text is implicit in its sections, while the sections nonetheless remain prominent individually (as is the case in even the most structured of quilts, my gardening/quilting friend Juliet reminds me).

There is now a long tradition of feminist texts composed or constructed as collections of short essays personal or informal in tone, sometimes interspersed with poems, talks, or interviews, rather than as a single, sustained argument. I see similar cross-threads behind, around, and through Rich's *On Lies, Secrets, and Silence* and *Blood, Bread, and Poetry,* Lorde's *Sister Outsider,* Bernikow's *Among Women,* Walker's *In Search of Our Mothers' Gardens,* Piercy's *Parti-Colored Blocks for a Quilt,* Gallagher's *Concert of Tenses,* Griffin's *Made from This Earth,* Gallop's *Thinking Through the Body,* Grahn's *Highest Apple,* Stimpson's *Where the Meanings Are,* Mairs's *Plaintext* and *Remembering the Bone House,* Anzaldúa's *Borderlands/La Frontera,* and Moraga's *Loving in the War Years,* as well as many works I've not been able to discuss in this study: Jordan's *Civil Wars* and *On Call,* Frye's *Politics of Reality,* Walker's *Living By the Word,* Rose's *Writing of Women,* and Maxine Kumin's *To Make a Prairie* and *In Deep,* to name perhaps only the most visible, oft-quoted, or well-published text(ualitie)s. There are more where these come from, and more to come. All of these are the sister-texts through and alongside which I find (or find again) my feminist poet-critic voice.[7]

"Closer Yet I Approach You":
Women Writing on Women in *Between Women*

Carol Ascher, Louise DeSalvo, and Sara Ruddick collaborated on *Between Women: Biographers, Novelists, Critics, Teachers and Artists Write about Their Work on Women*. In this 1984 anthology, women write about the collaborative spirit that often overtook them as they earlier wrote about, photographed, or produced other forms of art about specific women. Reading the collection, I was struck by two things. *Between Women* encouraged a discourse usually both more personal and more meta-discursive than the project about which the contributors were reporting. It was as if, instead of reacting "too personally" and then retreating into "professionalism," these women were doing the opposite—finally finding (or perhaps finding again) the personal, emotional bases and consequences of their work on women. Though doubling their distance from their alleged subjects, they were now even more subjective about or closer to them. As a reader at an even further remove from the subjects, I felt extremely engaged, though I found myself wishing the authors had written with this much intensity and autobiography in the first place (to be fair, some had, at least by their accounts), in which case I would have been more likely to look up the works to which these accounts refer.

The second thing that struck me was how strongly the writers took cues not only from the artists on whom they worked but from the editors who served as muses as they asked provocative questions about process and purpose: "How did their projects begin? Why did they turn to a woman or women for study? Who encouraged, who dispirited them? What did they hope their work would do for them or their readers? What doubts arose . . . ? How did they change in the course of their work? . . . Were they transformed as writers, activists, teachers, artists, lovers, mothers, daughters, feminists?" (xix–xx). Unlike Piercy, Gallagher, Walker, and Griffin, who modeled themselves on their mothers' arts or an earthy notion of organicism, these essayists got direction from editors, and the editors (who are also contributors) got help from other essayists' examples and from one another as well. These "cultivated" essays blossomed in ways both personal and formally (or better, informally) innovative. Their authors transformed themselves from scholars to writer-scholars or poet-scholars.

Myrtha Chabron, for example, writes a letter to her mother explaining the meaning of her work on Julia de Burgos. The letter crosses from English to Spanish, prose to poetry: "Roots. Nature. Landscape. I love to hear you talk about your childhood in Esperanza. . . . The writers I have been telling you about, mami, carry similar memories of the wild places where they grew up" (167–68); "the typography of our landscape becomes our skin" (169). Leah Blatt Glasser, among others, moves from a specific account of her scholarly project to an intellectual and familial autobiography accounting for both her emergence as a feminist scholar and her renewed appreciation and emulation of "the skill, the worth in those womanly tasks that would not [formerly] fit my sense of freedom" (Glasser, on Mary Wilkins Freeman, 200). Ascher, DeSalvo, and Ruddick put it this way:

> Several contributors reject both the style and the morality of the academic, publishing, and literary worlds. Women want to invent new types of criticism, alternative forms of cooperation. . . . Several ask that work be both more and less: less compulsive, aggressive, lonely, competitive; more communal, caring, and integrated with love and politics. . . . All of our essayists are aware that . . . their portraits are ultimately their creations—a blend of their subjects' lives and their own. . . . Certainly our book is an attempt, as one contributing editor put it, to "put the portrait painter into the painting." (xxii–xxv)

Between Women exemplifies well feminist reclamation and (re)generation. Moreover, there is at work what some feminists consider the inclusive logic of "both/and" rather than the sometimes divisive one of "either/or": recycling and reclaiming are both conservative (they conserve energy, are thrifty, and hold onto the past) and politically progressive ("liberal" or "progressive" municipalities are often the ones most committed to avoiding the waste of landscapes, seascapes, and expended energies through paper/aluminum/glass recycling).

Again the vocabulary of the homespun, of gardening and

making quilts, crops up. The collaborative introduction speaks of the idea for the collection having taken *root,* and describes how one essayist (Jane Marcus) "compares the retrieving of women's lives and the rereading of their texts to the '*invisible mending*' her mother and aunts engaged in, celebrating rather than repudiating our female heritage" (xxii; emphasis mine). Carol Ascher speaks of sometimes wishing her book on Simone de Beauvoir had a "clean, sleek surface . . . unbroken, invulnerable, unruffled by the squirms of a conflicted 'I'" (102), as if a book were either a lake or a bedspread. In the rest of her essay, where she reproduces part of "Clearing the Air—a Personal Word," a long letter to de Beauvoir she controversially inserted like "a sexy centerfold" in her book, she affirms the "broken" (yet pieced-together?) aspect of her text. She writes, "Emotionally, the letter was effective. Once I had written it, I continued working on the book with more fluidity and joy and an easier, warmer feeling toward Simone de Beauvoir" (96). She closes by imagining "a new aesthetic (and a new morality) in which people, including myself, are more at ease with closeness, with uncertainty about truth, and with the confusing mix of subject and object that constitutes what is finally there to be seen" (102). Composing across borders, composing organically, or writing as patchwork are the various ways I speak about and share what Ascher and her colleagues affirm and desire.

Gloria T. Hull, in her essay about writing on Alice Dunbar-Nelson, finds herself affirming a set of "fundamental tenets" similar in many ways to the compositional aesthetics of Ascher, Griffin, Walker, Rich, and others (Hull herself says she risks sounding too simple or repetitive because so much feminist theory echoes her approach):

> (1) everything about the subject is important for a total understanding and analysis of her life and work; (2) the proper scholarly stance is engaged rather than "objective"; (3) the personal (both the subject's and the critic's) *is* political; (4) description must be accompanied by analysis; (5) consciously maintaining at all times the angle of vision of a person who is both Black [Jewish? Chicana? etc.] and female is imperative; (6) being principled requires rigorous truthfulness and "telling it all"; (7) research/

criticism is not an academic/intellectual game, but a pursuit of
social meanings *rooted* in the "real world." (110; emphasis mine)

Hull characterizes much of what the poet-critics I describe
above embody if not announce, as well as what I see myself
rooting for (pun intended) in this study.

There are different routes to the "personal" and "engaged"
stance, the "pursuit of social meanings rooted in the 'real
world.'" Meredith Tax wrote about "obscure women, long dead,
who were socialists, feminists, and labor organizers before
World War I" in both a history book, *The Rising of the Women,*
and a novel, *Rivington Street.* In *Between Women,* she writes
that she "loved these women for their conflicts: between work
and love, politics and family, the feminist movement and the
labor movement, the joys of poetry and the discipline of anal-
ysis" (344). Through reams of direct quotations, she saw that
she could recycle (after much hard work and revision) what was
published history into a historical novel focused specifically on
Jews in the New York garment industry (352–54). Her recycling
or reclaiming is not simply a matter of turning historical notes
into a novel; it permeates Tax's avowed "pleasure in finding out
and re-creating the ways our grandmothers did their work:
washing clothes in a cold-water flat, working in garment facto-
ries, doing fine sewing by hand, as Ruby, one of [the] central
characters, does" (353). After citing a detailed passage from her
novel, Tax reveals a philosophy of composition derived directly
from her sisters and foremothers who sewed: "Including such
details is a way of giving value for money. A book should be well
made, like a good coat. . . . If the style is too extreme or fanciful,
women won't be able to wear it for every day. I want to write
books simple enough for everyday use but strong enough to be
passed around from friend to relation, mother to daughter, and
even to be read more than once and to outlast current fashions"
(354).

The essay most focused on the idea of the homespun (or
better, home sewn) is Jane Marcus's "Invisible Mending." Al-
though Marcus at one point recognizes she had long been like
Dee/Wangero of Walker's story "Everyday Use"—as her moth-

er's less "loyal" daughter, she had gone off to Radcliffe over the protests of her mother and the nuns at her Catholic high school, her mother ever after feeling "patronized by [her] 'Radcliffe accent'" (394)—in writing this essay, she finds herself more deeply connected to her mother than is her Maggie-like sister, who was the once-proud recipient of "grandmother's Irish cut glass" celery dish, but who nonetheless sold it at a garage sale (394). Marcus begins with that new-felt connection: "Why . . . has it taken me so long to see the connections between my work, feminist criticism and biography, and my mother's work, 'invisible mending'?" She finds that "invisible mending has now become for [her] a metaphor for the feminist criticism our collective produces. We want to weave women's lives and works back into the fabric of culture, as if they had never been rent" (381). Beyond this, as Marcus herself confides, she wants to weave her own life into her work, "in the hope that in the process of reweaving the threads of [her] life, it may help other women make sense of their lives and work" (382). She is convinced, as I and so many members of a growing feminist collective are, that "the very telling of our stories helps us onward" (392).

In telling the story of her early and later schooling, Marcus weaves in the women she admired and admires for both their art and their lives: she says she "scrimped to save the money to buy a Marimekko dress solely because [she] saw Adrienne Rich, pregnant poet, pushing a baby carriage down Brattle Street in one" (386). She describes her growth as/into a feminist critic, from her early admiration for Amy Lowell (scoffed at by male college professors), her associating her mother's "invisible mending" with Ibsen's *A Doll's House* (because of Nora's fine-sewing through the nights), to her epiphanic hearing of papers on Virginia Woolf (how she came to join the "sisterhood of scholarship in Virginia Woolf studies"), and her realization of how much her life and work owe to Marie Bashkirtseff's diary, the memoirs of Sophie Kovalevsky, and Jane Ellen Harrison's *Reminiscence*. Marcus is careful to add, however, "But it is not only the life stories of heroines and great women that we need. Woolf thanks ordinary women, *like ourselves,* for adding to the collective history that allows us to 'think back through our mothers'"

(394; emphasis mine). So she links the scholarly piecework (book reviews and essays) she did when unable to find a full-time position to the sewn piecework her mother used to do for small amounts of money (388). And, still using the matrix or metaphors of her mother, Marcus wonders whether our feminist literary critical efforts will be "as lost to our descendants as the work of earlier feminist critics has been lost to us" (393) and as her mother's skills might be lost in one generation (396): "Is this whole process doomed like housework to go on forever? Will they always be ripping holes in our work, leaving us to sew them up again, always rending while we are mending?" (393).

If Marcus doesn't end completely hopefully, she does close with statements of connection, determination, and a plea: "We are not as different from working-class women as we sometimes think. Because we want to make the holes invisible in the fabric of society, we must keep our pens and needles sharp against the cloak of invisibility that our culture would still like to fling over us" (395). We must keep stitching, reclaiming, recycling, transforming as we think back through our mothers and work our way forward to and through the materials of our own lives and (border-crossing) feminist scholarship, theory, criticism. Or, put another way, cycling back to the poet-critic whose words begin this treatise, Adrienne Rich: "Begin with the material. Pick up again the long struggle against lofty and privileged abstraction. Perhaps this is the core of the revolutionary process" ("Notes towards a Politics of Location," *BBP* 213).

And so I assert and insert materials from my own life, materials that, although textual or linguistic—and thereby a kind of abstraction when compared with gardens and quilts—are nonetheless full of "concrete" diction, sensory detail. What, in words anyway, could be more down-to-earth than that? Texts are finally not immaterial. They spell freedom, allowing us to name adversaries, posit remedies, work toward connections and collaborations. But I remember as well Mary Daly's observation that the word *text,* like *texture,* comes from the Latin term *texere,* "to weave" (4). And feminist poet-critics, who seek to bridge poetry and criticism, the personal and the professional, writer and reader, seek also to weave together home and book, to make material all kinds of material, to spur and display the growth of women's culture.

I engage in what Rachel Blau DuPlessis might call a "poetics of interested meditation" offering "situational, dialogic, and lyrical statements" (*Writing Beyond the Ending* ix) because poet-critics like Adrienne Rich call for such a personal, material engagement, and because I admire the examples of Griffin, Walker, Gallagher, Anzaldúa, Lorde, Bernikow, and those other self-conscious, self-declaring feminists who seek a seamless continuity between their writing and their lives and who advocate a poetics of inclusion—of others' lives and words, not only their own; of poetry as much as prose; of intuition, angst, and cheer as much as analysis. I take to heart Rich's aesthetic of beginning with "the geography closest in—the body," because, as Susan Griffin's interviewee K. L. understood, we know that we exist only by acknowledging, knowing our bodies. And so I began by talking about my bodily—and intellectual, yes—harassment in the academy and my search for remedy in language close to me, in poet-critics who I felt were close to me. And yet not me. "We who are many and do not want to be the same" (Rich, *BBP* 225) and who even as individuals are many, manifold, a crosshatch or quilt of identities, changeable, remediable, readable—like our perhaps bodily and situationally inspired prose.

In order to talk about border crossers and writers from other places, other ethnicities, races, religions, and classes than my own, I felt I must be willing to confide who, what, and where I think I am or have been as I cross and blend genres in defiance of some critical conventions and in emulation and yet renovation of others. Defining my textual, writerly identity always in the context of, in relation to, others (as Abel, Barker-Nunn, Chodorow, and others would have it), I am in a unique position to follow the textual process by which representative poet-critics find theirs (in group process, claims Piercy; upon my entrance into the feminist, notes Griffin; torn among cultures, languages, genres, implies Anzaldúa).

In "The Critic as Feminist: Reflections on Women's Poetry,

Feminism and the Art of Criticism," Suzanne Juhasz explains, and I agree, that "the inclusion of the personal, the individual, and the subjective within the act of criticism is a response on the part of feminist critics to, first of all, the art by women which has been our subject. Secondly it is a response to the limited procedures of the profession as we have perceived them" (126). I wrote earlier that I believe in responding in kind, in performative rhetoric, in practicing what I praise. In the end, I have sought to acclaim but also to claim for myself the power of feminists' critical-autobiographical-poetic amalgams, their creative alchemy, their "will to change," to reclaim the title of one of Adrienne Rich's books of poems.

Afterwords

When I was young and growing up in Long Island, I couldn't adjust to the changes of seasons very well. Spring would come and the trees would unfurl their fisted leaves, our magenta azaleas would blaze, but I'd be wearing a knit hat with a built-in hairband holder at the front and a dangling tassel at the back. I was not only strongly habituated to certain temperatures, but too loyal to certain clothes as well. I'd resist changing. I wanted to wear that hat. When I insisted that my mother buy me D-width shoes with double T-straps because I could barely stand to have even these wide shoes touching my feet, she complied even though she thought (rightly, as it turns out) my feet would stretch out and be forever hard to fit. For years I would wear only that particular style of shoes, fussing and fuming when I was too big for the bright-white, double-strapped, children's shoe.

In my later youth, still afraid of change in general (as represented by the butterfly, which emerges from its cocoon different from how it began), I wrote:

The Butterfly

At the shaky age of ten,
I was given a blue bicycle.
Twelve years later, it shakes—as if in memory.

A butterfly assaulted me like a man
with a stocking over his tongue;
I shouted and swerved.

Just last week, I counted ten
caterpillars on the worn stone path
by the river in the woods.

This morning's yellow wings are new and
like two thousand strings filling in
a harp,

so compacted
they remain silent even when
vibrating.

Butterflies always make me skittery.

This yellow, broken-winged bird
eats nothing and flies askew
while a sparrow or an eagle eats ten times

its weight.
I was bird-boned at ten, fifty thin pounds,
but I didn't eat.

I don't belong bicycling,
fearing the feather flying of any moth,
shaking so easily.

By the side-of-the-road lilies,
I hid my face from the zig zag motion
of change.

Even as a grownup I find I'm not the adjustable type. As I
wrote in a recent essay ostensibly about my difficulty adjusting
to wearing glasses, when I moved to my new house I couldn't
adjust to the change of address. I didn't just mean the street and
number (I'd stayed in the same city) but the address my body
made to the kitchen sink, the new distance between stove and
refrigerator, the change in the place where I stored my clothes,
sleeping with my head north instead of west, the dishes sud-
denly east, and so forth. Neither arrangement, old or new, was
more practical than the other; I just didn't like any kind of
change, inside the house or out. I disliked going to a new grocery
store where I couldn't find my brand of granola bars, found it
uncomfortable riding a new bus. (I then remembered that in
high school I insisted on sitting always in the same seat, alone,
at the back of the bus, often fighting with another girl—Fe-
lice?—who also claimed to like the seat). I've had the same
hairstyle for years—long, uncomplicated. And I tended to flat-

ten out the seasons when I lived in Seattle by insisting on doing my running in shorts and T-shirt, whatever the weather or time of year, though I'd don gloves, thick socks, and an earband when the wind blew.

So now, I'm wondering, how did I come to advocate writing with an allegiance to the seasons, writing out of a changing body a flexible and fluid prose? I suppose it's because this malleable, cross-genre writing often grounds itself in the familiar, a familiar body or body of works, familiar landscapes and seascapes, familiar and friendly tones. Offering as they do the compensatory experience of a succession of blooms, gardens are especially useful for helping my stuck self adjust to changing seasons. At my Seattle house, the bushes and blooms were familiar in both their recurrence and their type, because I recognized them and because so many looked like the ones my mother grows: my mother has azaleas of exactly the same magenta as mine, growing just like mine did out front, next to clumps of purple irises. What my mother didn't have, my garden also compensated and carried on for: her wisteria wouldn't bloom; mine did. She didn't have lilacs.

Once I got the garden going at my new house, once the pets and photographs and favorite books were back inside, I could create and weave and nurture this text, sitting at my old desk and watching out the window the lilacs bloom.

Notes

Works Cited

Index

Notes

Chapter One: Discourse as Power

1. See also Judith Kegan Gardiner, "On Female Identity and Writing by Women," and Sandra Gilbert, "Feminist Criticism in the University: An Interview with Sandra Gilbert." Feminist poet-critics not only write literary and cultural criticism in the female mode, however; their poetic, reader-oriented, autobiographical writing characteristically blurs and crosses genres, as I discuss at greater length in subsequent chapters.

2. As Hélène Cixous writes in "Reaching a Point of Wheat, or, Portrait of the Artist as a Maturing Woman," "Everytime I say 'masculine' or 'feminine,' or 'man' or 'woman' [or 'male' or 'female'], please use as many quotation marks as you need to avoid taking these terms too literally" (1). "Male" here is to be equated with conventional academic discourse, that which Mary DeShazer describes as "formal, detached, pontifical" (118), Thomas J. Farrell as "framed" or "contained" (910), and Pamela Annas as "linear," "logical," "objective," and "abstract" (360). See also Clara Juncker, "Writing (with) Cixous."

3. I find very useful here Jerome Bruner's distinction between *paradigmatic* and *narrative* modes of thought, the one "seeking generality and the second uniqueness," as Mary Field Belenky et al. sum up in *Women's Ways of Knowing* (113 n.2). Belenky and her coauthors speak of "connected knowers" as those who learn that "if one can discover the experimental logic behind . . . ideas, the ideas become less strange and the owners of ideas cease to be strangers"; their empathy makes possible an expanded "experiential base" and expanded knowledge (115). Combining Bruner and Belenky et al., I call this learning and knowing through others' and one's own stories "narrative knowing."

4. I heard this commonsense view of the aftermath of child abuse on a television talk show sometime in 1989.

5. See note 3 above and also Barbara Ryan, "Chrysalis: A Thesis Journal," in which Ryan asserts that a thesis or literary-critical endeavor "is also, inevitably, a kind of story, and that my thesis will be a

story of my own involvement in particular kinds of female experience and its representation" (4).

6. Recounted in Marilyn Frye, "On Being White: Thinking toward a Feminist Understanding of Race and Race Supremacy," in *The Politics of Reality: Essays in Feminist Theory,* 112.

7. In her introduction to Grahn's book of poems *The Work of a Common Woman,* Rich writes, "The 'Common Woman' is far more than a class description. What is 'common' in and to women is the intersection of oppression and strength, damage and beauty. It is, quite simply, the *ordinary* in women which will 'rise' in every sense of the word—spiritually and in activism. . . . Grahn reclaims 'the common woman' as a phrase from simplistic Marxist associations, or such political clichés as 'the century of the common man'" (17–18).

8. See, for example, Hélène Cixous, "The Laugh of the Medusa"; Luce Irigaray, *Speculum of the Other Woman* and *The Sex Which Is Not One;* and the Elaine Marks and Isabelle de Courtivron anthology, *New French Feminisms.*

9. More than merely celebrating the end of denial, I intended my chapter subtitle as an ironic reminder that we need to be ever more self-aware. Just when we think we are practicing what we preach, we may catch ourselves doing otherwise; we "renounce [or deny] denial" (that is, we are still caught in the denial trap) when we might be affirming alternatives.

10. "Sonnet," a "little song" (*Webster's Third New International Dictionary*) or a "dim[inutive] of *suono* sound," was early any short poem (*Oxford English Dictionary*).

11. Piercy, who writes poetry and both fictional and nonfictional prose, speaks of the "intensity of poetry" versus the "roominess of prose" (*PCB* 193).

12. See Gardiner, "On Female Identity," and those works on which she draws: Nancy Chodorow, *The Reproduction of Mothering,* and Sara Ruddick, "Maternally Thinking."

Chapter Two: Border Crossing as Method and Motif

1. I was going to write, "which are the 'true' subject of this chapter," only to realize there are in fact several subjects and subjectivities cross-hatching here. In *Thinking Through the Body,* Jane Gallop takes Freud as one of her central subjects, subjecting him to a reading that wonderfully underscores my reading of his editor's footnote. According to Gallop, Freud's work (like the paraphernalia surrounding or extending it that I examine here) "calls into question the neat distinction between science and poetry . . . objectivity and subjectivity, theory and

intimacy" (6). A combination of his work and that of Roland Barthes and Adrienne Rich authorized Gallop's "own push out of objective, scholarly discourse into something more embodied" (11). I have come to see that Freud/my reading of the Freudian text and now Gallop (along with Rich, Anzaldúa, Moraga, and Kingston) similarly authorize my pushing at the (seeming) borders of books, genres, and self to blend "theory and intimacy," analysis and poetry, autobiography and literary criticism.

2. Rich is now an affiliated or self-identified Jew; she married a Jew, raised her sons as Jews, and writes or speaks out of an ever-sharper Jewish identity. See *Blood, Bread, and Poetry* and her most recent books of poetry.

3. Perhaps this further explains the perhaps well-meaning but sometimes wrongheaded tendency of (white) feminists like myself to confuse our individual experiences with those of another. At times, co-(r)responding with another may be appropriate; at others, it suggests an act of appropriation or even colonization. I would, however, prefer to think of a writer who is able to reach beyond her text to her reader as making a friendly advance, helping to build a collaborative challenge to conventional hierarchies and exclusions in critical prose—and in the world.

4. They may also challenge domineering women and their words, but since men hold the power in patriarchy, the critic who bards over/lords over others is gendered "male."

5. Some of the legacies feminist quilt or collage form shares with postmodern and other experiments with bricolage or border crossing are addressed in chapter 3.

6. In her refusal to split parts of herself or spheres of her life, Anzaldúa may also be drawing on what lesbian poet-critic Judy Grahn considers a legacy of Sappho: "We do not take the sacred, the political, the social, the details of everyday, and carry them 'away' or split them from each other. We place them all together in the real lives of real women in the present, in the raucous, dangerous, and tumultuous marketplace/urban/warzone/suburb of modern life. Sappho did" (*Highest Apple* 88).

7. See Maxine Hairston, "The Winds of Change: Thomas Kuhn and the Revolution in the Teaching of Writing," and Kuhn's own work, *The Structure of Scientific Revolutions*.

8. Besides those writers with at least occasional connections to English and other literature departments, writing conferences, and the like (including Rich, Anzaldúa, Moraga, Kingston, Tompkins, Piercy, Grahn, Gallagher, Griffin, and Gilbert), I think here of philosopher-writer Marilyn Frye (*The Politics of Reality*) and sociologist-autobiographer Anne Oakley (*Taking It Like a Woman*), among others. Like

Gilbert, I feel that "perhaps the poet-critic will be revived [is revived], then, in a role far more ancient . . . than that of theorist: the role of prophetess or prophet" ("Interview" 122).

9. See Juliet Mitchell and Jacqueline Rose, eds., *Feminine Sexuality: Jacques Lacan and the Ecole Freudienne,* esp. 6 and 32, and Jacques Lacan, *Ecrits: A Selection.* I am indebted also to Steven Shaviro for my reading of Lacan.

10. To be more accurate, I should note that Anzaldúa refers to, if not employs, some eight languages spoken by her people. They are: standard English, working-class and slang English, standard Spanish, standard Mexican Spanish, north Mexican Spanish dialect, Chicano Spanish with its regional variations, Tex-Mex, and *Pachuco* or *calo.* She points to the Chicano penchant for "switching codes": "We speak a patois, a forked tongue, a variation of two languages" (55).

11. For this notion, Jean Barker-Nunn, like Judith Kegan Gardiner, whom I've quoted earlier, is indebted to the theories of Nancy Chodorow and Carol Gilligan. See Chodorow, *The Reproduction of Mothering,* and Gilligan, *In a Different Voice: Psychological Theory and Women's Development.*

12. See King-Kok Cheung, " 'Don't Tell': Imposed Silences in *The Color Purple* and *The Woman Warrior.*"

Chapter Three: Con-text/uality

1. For similar overviews of feminist criticism, see Toril Moi, *Sexual/Textual Politics,* and Janet Todd, *Feminist Literary History,* especially their respective introductions. Despite their disavowal of binary splits, many critical historians of the feminist/poststructuralist continuum—even those who focus on the differences *within* feminist or poststructuralist literary criticism(s)—imply that given thinkers either line up more closely to one pole than the other or that they are preoccupied (as the historians themselves are) with the question of the compatibility of "two views"—the authority or authenticity of the author versus his/her construction/deconstruction through discourse. Moi, for example, as Maggie Humm aptly notes, derogates "Anglo-American criticism as if it were a homogeneous entity. . . . Moi unfairly attacks Anglo-Americans as humanist empiricists" (113 n.1). (It's tempting to oversimplify. I myself adopt at times an either/or perspective in order to tease out what I consider the very real possibilities of a dialectical or dialogic feminist criticism that operates in the confluence of a variety of recent theories of language, self, ideology. See my discussion of Catherine Stimpson's *Where the Meanings Are* in the section on Salman Rushdie.)

2. Fuller accounts of the rioting taking place over the book, the deaths in the street, and the three-million-dollar reward offered for Rushdie's murder were carried in the *New York Times* on 19 February 1989 and in other newspapers of that date and thereafter. The television show I saw aired on 27 February 1989.

3. Composition theorist Peter Elbow echoed my sentiment when he declared "the primary relation most academics have to academic discourse is a sense of duty" ("Problematics of Academic Discourse"). Yet trying to write otherwise while needing to be taken seriously in the academy is no easy thing.

4. While many members of PEN hold academic positions, many (other) academics do not write regularly in creative, personal, or potentially subversive forms.

5. In her review of Daphne Patai's *Brazilian Women Speak: Contemporary Life Stories,* Linda Rabben suggests that the vast majority of Brazilian women not only have no voice but no sense of a "life story" at all, no sense of self the way we define it in the U.S. "Some cultures scarcely have room for the concept of a self," Rabben continues (15). See also Rich's discussion of—and notes regarding—the "cramp[ing] of [female] creativeness" in her essay "Compulsory Heterosexuality and Lesbian Existence" (*BBP* 38).

6. Bella Brodzki and Celeste Schenck comment in *Life/Lines: Theorizing Women's Autobiography* (1988) that "the duplicitous and complicitious relationship of 'life' and 'art' in autobiographical modes is precisely the point. To elide it in the name of eliminating the 'facile assumption of referentiality' is dangerously to ignore the crucial referentiality of class, race, and sexual orientation; it is to beg serious political questions" (12–13).

7. Such not-genres are akin to what Sandra Gilbert, in "The American Sexual Poetics of Walt Whitman and Emily Dickinson," calls the "not poetry" of Whitman and Dickinson (128), their production of a new kind of literature that went against, in Whitman's words, "the confectioners and upholsterers of verse" (131) by drawing on—in Whitman's case—journalism, American oratory, biblical rhetoric, and "even . . . popular domestic and melodramatic fiction," and—in Dickinson's case—hymnals, epitaphs, children's rhymes, and the conventions of female letter writing and the themes of women's fiction (133).

8. The year 1973 seems to have been the watershed for consciousness-raising (CR) groups. See Claudia Dreifus, Marilyn Frye, Susan Jacoby, Anica Mander, Sheila Ruth, and a host of others for accounts of such group phenomena ranging from old friends "supporting one another in a new experience: an effort to expand their middle-aged lives beyond the comfortable roles of wife, mother and grandmother" (Jacoby 10) to (an ultimately problematical) "consciousness-raising group to identify

and explore the racism in our lives with a view to dismantling the barriers that blocked our understanding and action in this matter" (Frye 110) to CR as part of psychotherapy (Mander) from the seventies to the present.

9. In *Women of Academe: Outsiders in the Sacred Grove,* co-editors Nadya Aisenberg and Mona Harrington compile interviews with sixty academic women and examine women's "struggle to gain authority in the academic profession and to use that authority to change conventional practices" (bookjacket).

10. I would add that the language of common speech was a topic later addressed by Rich, Griffin, Grahn, Piercy, and others as well.

11. The project description comes from a flier we circulated calling for papers for a collection whose early working title was "In Our Own Voices: Feminist Forms of Literary Criticism."

12. See David Bleich, *Subjective Criticism;* Keith Fort, "Form, Authority, and the Critical Essay"; Elizabeth Flynn, "Composing as a Woman" and "Composing Responses to Literary Texts: A Process Approach"; Nancy Jo Hoffman, "Reading Women's Poetry: The Meaning of Our Lives"; Charles Moran, "Teaching Writing/Teaching Literature"; Bruce Peterson, "Writing about Responses: A Unified Model of Reading, Interpretation, and Composition"; Anthony Petrosky, "From Story to Essay"; and Mariolina Salvatori, "Reading and Writing a Text: Correlations Between Reading and Writing Patterns."

13. There are exceptions, of course—those critic-theorists who practice what they preach, as it were. See, for example, Norman Holland's "Transacting My 'Good-Morrow' or, Bringing Back the Vanished Critic," and Ihab Hassan's "Parabiography: The Varieties of Critical Experience," both in Victor Kramer, ed., *American Critics at Work.* Holland makes his personal presence known in every paragraph ("As I read them"; "If I continue associating"), while Hassan gives biographical details about himself in the third person while theorizing about (auto)biography and criticism.

14. As Robert Scholes puts it, "implicit throughout [*Textual Power*] is the notion that reading and writing are important because we read and write our world as well as our texts, and are read and written by them in turn" (xi).

15. Jane Gallop is perhaps instead an Emersonian kind of poet for whom it was not "meter" but a "meter-making argument" that made poetry or poets. In any case, her work, with its informality, sexual frankness, and playful punning, inspiringly challenges critical conventions.

16. I am referring to Rich, Walker, Gallagher, Piercy, Maxine Kumin, and others—poets whose prose is not only typically more intimate than Arnold's, Eliot's, or Derrida's, but whose writing draws on

ordinary letters, not merely "belles lettres." See, for example, "Women of Letters," in Marge Piercy's *Twelve-Spoked Wheel Flashing* (54–57). See also my allusion to Peter Elbow's letter writing in the next paragraph.

17. All these writers speak against "logic" and frankly for and from the body and their own lives. See especially Barthes, *Roland Barthes par roland barthes;* Hélène Cixous, "Sorties: Out and Out: Attacks/ Ways Out/Forays"; and Luce Irigaray, *This Sex Which Is Not One.*

18. Even some nonfeminist theorists, from Harold Bloom to Robert Scholes, seem to agree. Bloom considers each poem a response to earlier poems, while Scholes asserts that "the response to a text is always a text" (*Textual Power* 20). Barbara Ryan undertakes an exciting, full-length version of reflexive and reflective responding-in-kind in "Chrysalis: A Thesis Journal." Like the journals Ryan writes about, her writing has "a shape of its own, a shape that was curved rather than linear. It wasn't an argument." It "developed as a spiral, balanced deeply within itself and growing by addition at the open end" (from her dissertation abstract).

Chapter Four: The Ecology of Alchemy

1. For variations on this theme, see, for example, Sylvia Plath's "Stillborn," "Barren Woman," "Nick and the Candlestick," and "Child" (*The Collected Poems*), and Anne Sexton's "Ghosts," "The Black Art," and "Uterus" (*The Complete Poems*).

2. In "Fame, Fortune, and Other Tawdry Illusions," Piercy notes that once in a woman's workshop at a writing conference, "several of the mothers were talking about feeling guilty about the time they took to write, time taken from spending with their children." When Piercy asked one who had been widely published whether being paid for her work didn't lessen the guilt, the mother-writer agreed (*PCB* 230).

3. Diane Wakoski sees the connection I do, calling Piercy "truly a daughter of Whitman . . . in spite of urban origins . . . she has found a pure American identity in her body, her geography, landscape, and the knowledge which comes from these things" (7). Upon reading a draft of this chapter, Piercy wrote to me, "I would cite Emily Dickinson equally with Whitman as my earliest influences and possibly the most powerful" (letter to the author, 15 Jan. 1991).

4. Perhaps a further demonstration of the quiltlike or (re)generational in Gallagher is the part of her essay that closes with the whiff of the poststructural about it—"They did not truly exist until this writing" (23).

5. Walker here quotes from her own foreword to Robert Hemen-

way, *Zora Neale Hurston: A Literary Biography* (Urbana: U of Illinois P, 1977).

6. See Yeats's "Dialogue of Self and Soul" or Marvell's "Dialogue between the Soul and Body," widely available in collections such as *The Norton Anthology of Modern Poetry* or *The Norton Anthology of Poetry*.

7. See also *The Intimate Critique,* edited by Diane Freedman, Olivia Frey, and Frances Zauhar, for its bibliography of autobiographical, genre-crossing literary criticism. Two of the most recent entries are Nicole Ward Jouve's *White Woman Speaks with Forked Tongue: Criticism as Autobiography,* and Nancy K. Miller's *Getting Personal,* both of which were published as this book went to press.

Works Cited

Abel, Elizabeth. "(E)merging Identities: The Dynamics of Female Friendship in Contemporary Fiction by Women." *Signs* 6.3 (Spring 1981): 413–35.

Aisenberg, Nadya, and Mona Harrington, eds. *Women of Academe: Outsiders in the Sacred Grove.* Amherst: U of Massachusetts P, 1988.

Allegro, Peggy. "The Strange and the Familiar: The Evolutionary Potential of Lesbianism." *The Lesbian Reader.* Ed. Gina Covina and Laurel Galana. Oakland, Calif., Amazon, 1975. 167–84.

Allen, Paula Gunn. *The Sacred Hoop: Recovering the Feminine in American Indian Traditions.* Boston: Beacon, 1986.

Altieri, Charles. Class lecture, University of Washington. 29 Mar. 1989.

Anderson, Linda. "At the Threshold of the Self: Women and Autobiography." *Women's Writing: A Challenge to Theory.* Ed. Moira Monteith. New York: St. Martin's, 1986. 54–70.

Annas, Pamela. "Silences: Women's Language Research and the Teaching of Writing." *Teaching Writing: Pedagogy, Gender, and Equity.* Ed. Cynthia Caywood and Gillian R. Overing. Albany: SUNY P, 1987. 3–17.

———. "Style as Politics: A Feminist Approach to the Teaching of Writing." *College English* 47 (1985): 360–71.

Anzaldúa, Gloria. *Borderlands/La Frontera.* San Francisco: Spinsters–Aunt Lute, 1987.

Ascher, Carol, Louise DeSalvo, and Sara Ruddick, eds. *Between Women: Biographers, Novelists, Critics, Teachers and Artists Write about Their Work on Women.* Boston: Beacon, 1984.

Baker, Houston. Introduction. *Narrative of the Life of Frederick Douglass, an American Slave.* By Frederick Douglass. Ed. Houston Baker. New York: Penguin, 1982.

———. "Theory and Poetics of Afro-American Women's Writing." Hilen Memorial Lecture. Department of English, University of Washington. 5 Nov. 1987.

Barker-Nunn, Jean. "Telling the Mother's Story: History and Connection in the Autobiographies of Maxine Hong Kingston and Kim Chernin." *Women's Studies* 14 (July 1987): 56–63.

Barthes, Roland. "The Death of the Author." *Image-Music-Text.* Trans. Stephen Heath. New York: Hill and Wang, 1977. 142–48.

———. *Roland Barthes par roland barthes.* Paris: Seuil, 1975.

Belenky, Mary Field, Blythe McVicker Clinchy, Nancy Rule Goldberger, and Jill Mattuck Tarule. *Women's Ways of Knowing: The Development of Self, Voice, and Mind.* New York: Basic, 1986.

Bernikow, Louise. *Among Women.* New York: Harper, 1980.

Bishop, Elizabeth. "Faustina, or, Rock Roses." *The Complete Poems, 1927–1979.* New York: Farrar, 1983. 72.

Bleich, David. *Subjective Criticism.* Baltimore: Johns Hopkins UP, 1978.

Brill, A. A. Introduction. *The Basic Writings of Sigmund Freud.* By Sigmund Freud. Ed. A. A. Brill. New York: Random, 1938. 3–32.

Brodzki, Bella, and Celeste Schenck, eds. *Life/Lines: Theorizing Women's Autobiography.* Ithaca: Cornell UP, 1988.

Brownstein, Rachel M. *Becoming a Heroine: Reading about Women in Novels.* New York: Viking-Penguin, 1982.

Bruss, Elizabeth. *Beautiful Theories: The Spectacle of Discourse in Contemporary Criticism.* Baltimore: Johns Hopkins UP, 1982.

Caywood, Cynthia, and Gillian R. Overing, eds. *Teaching Writing: Gender, Pedagogy, and Equity.* Albany: SUNY P, 1987.

Chapman, Irv. "Mario Baeza: A Corporate Lawyer's Life." *Cornell '88* Spring 1988: 11.

Cheung, King-Kok. " 'Don't Tell': Imposed Silences in *The Color Purple* and *The Woman Warrior.*" *PMLA* 103.2 (1988): 162–74.

Chodorow, Nancy. *The Reproduction of Mothering: Psychoanalysis and the Sociology of Gender.* Berkeley: U of California P, 1978.

Christian, Barbara. *Black Feminist Criticism.* New York: Pergamon, 1985.

Cixous, Hélène. "Castration or Decapitation?" Trans. Annette Kuhn. *Signs* 7.11 (Autumn 1981): 41–55.

———. "The Laugh of the Medusa." *New French Feminisms: An Anthology.* Ed. Elaine Marks and Isabelle de Courtivron. Amherst: U of Massachusetts P, 1980. 245–65.

———. "Reaching the Point of Wheat, or, Portrait of the Artist as a Maturing Woman." *New Literary History* 19.1 (Fall 1987): 1–22.

———. "Sorties: Out and Out: Attacks/Ways Out/Forays." *The Newly Born Woman.* Trans. Betsy Wing. Minneapolis: U of Minnesota P, 1986. 558–78.

Clifford, James, and George E. Marcus. *Writing Culture: The Poetics and Politics of Ethnography.* Berkeley and Los Angeles: U of California P, 1986.

Cott, Nancy. "Feminist Theory and Feminist Movements: The Past Before Us." *What is Feminism?* Ed. Juliet Mitchell and Ann Oakley. New York: Pantheon, 1986. 49–62.

Daly, Mary. *Gyn/Ecology: The Metaethics of Radical Feminism.* Boston: Beacon, 1978.

Deleuze, Gilles, and Felix Guattari. *Anti-Oedipus: Capitalism and Schizophrenia.* Trans. Robert Hurley et al. New York: Viking, 1977.

———. *A Thousand Plateaus: Capitalism and Schizophrenia.* Trans. Brian Massumi. Minneapolis: U of Minnesota P, 1987.

DeMan, Paul. "Semiology and Rhetoric." *Textual Strategies.* Ed. Josue V. Harari. Ithaca: Cornell UP, 1979. 121–40.

DeShazer, Mary. "Creation and Relation: Teaching Essays by T. S. Eliot and Adrienne Rich." *Teaching Writing: Pedagogy, Gender, and Equity.* Ed. Cynthia Caywood and Gillian R. Overing. Albany: SUNY P, 1987. 113–22.

Dickinson, Emily. *The Complete Poems.* Ed. Thomas H. Johnson. Boston: Little, 1960.

Dillard, Annie. "To Fashion a Text." *Inventing the Truth: The Art and Craft of Memoir.* Ed. William Zinsser. Boston: Houghton, 1987. 53–76.

Donne, John. "Meditation XVII." *Norton Anthology of Literature,* 3d ed. New York: Norton, 1974. 1:1215.

Dreifus, Claudia. *Women's Fate: Raps from a Feminist CR Group.* New York: Bantam, 1973.

DuPlessis, Rachel Blau. *The Pink Guitar: Writing as Feminist Practice.* New York and London: Routledge, 1990.

———. *Writing Beyond the Ending: Narrative Strategies of Twentieth-Century Women Writers.* Bloomington: Indiana UP, 1985.

Eagleton, Terry. *Literary Theory.* Minneapolis: U of Minnesota P, 1983.

Edwards, Lee. "Self Assertions." Rev. of *Life/Lines: Theorizing Women's Autobiographies,* ed. Bella Brodzki and Celeste Schenck (Cornell, 1988), and *The Private Self: Theory and*

Practice of Women's Autobiographical Writings, ed. Shari Benstock (U of North Carolina P, 1988). *Women's Review of Books* 6.6 (Mar. 1989): 7–8.

Elbow, Peter. "The Problematics of Academic Discourse." Conference on College Composition and Communication. Seattle, 17 Mar. 1989.

———. "Reflections on Academic Discourse: How It Relates to Freshmen and Colleagues." *College English* 53.2 (Feb. 1991): 135–55.

Emerson, Ralph Waldo. "The Poet." *Selected Writings of Ralph Waldo Emerson.* Ed. William H. Gilman. New York: New Signet–American Library, 1985. 306–27.

Far, Sui Sin [Edith Maud Eaton]. "Leaves from the Mental Portfolio of a Eurasian." *The Ethnic American Woman: Problems, Protests, Lifestyles.* Ed. Edith Blicksilver. Dubuque, Iowa: Kendall/Hunt, 1978. 187–89.

Farrell, Thomas J. "Male and Female Modes of Discourse." *College English* 40 (1979): 922–27.

Fetterley, Judith. Introduction. *Provisions: A Reader from Nineteenth-Century American Women.* Ed. Judith Fetterley. Bloomington: Indiana UP, 1985.

Flynn, Elizabeth. "Composing as a Woman." *College Composition and Communication* 39.4 (Dec. 1988): 423–35.

———. "Composing Responses to Literary Texts: A Process Approach." *College Composition and Communication* 34 (Oct. 1983): 342–48.

Fort, Keith. "Form, Authority, and the Critical Essay." *Contemporary Rhetoric.* Ed. W. Ross Winterowd. New York: Harcourt, 1975.

Foucault, Michel. "What Is an Author?" *Textual Strategies.* Ed. Josue V. Harari. Ithaca: Cornell UP, 1979. 141–60.

Freedman, Diane. "The Butterfly." *Transition* (Spring 1979): 19.

———. "Case Studies and Trade Secrets: Allaying Student Fears in the 'Litcomp' Classroom." *College Literature* 18.1 (Feb. 1991): 77–83.

———. "The Performance." *Permafrost* 7.1–2 (Spring 1985): 36.

———. "The Way the Gravestones Align: Ithaca, NY/ Shamokin, PA." *Matrix. University of Washington Daily* 9 May 1985: 7.

Freedman, Diane, Olivia Frey, and Frances Zauhar, eds. *The Intimate Critique: Autobiographical Literary Criticism.* Durham: Duke UP, forthcoming.

Frost, Robert. "Education by Poetry." *Norton Reader.* 6th ed. New York: Norton, 1984. 1025–33.

Frye, Marilyn. *The Politics of Reality: Essays in Feminist Theory.* Freedom, Calif.: Crossing, 1983.

Gallagher, Tess. *A Concert of Tenses: Essays on Poetry.* Ann Arbor: U of Michigan P, 1986.

Gallop, Jane. *Thinking Through the Body.* New York: Columbia UP, 1988.

Gardiner, Judith Kegan. "On Female Identity and Writing by Women." *Writing and Sexual Difference.* Ed. Elizabeth Abel. Chicago: U of Chicago P, 1982. 177–92.

Gates, Henry Louis, Jr. Introduction. *The Classic Slave Narratives.* Ed. Henry Louis Gates, Jr. New York: Penguin, 1987.

Geertz, Clifford. "Blurred Genres: The Refiguration of Social Thought." *Local Knowledge: Further Essays in Interpretive Anthropology.* New York: Basic, 1983. 19–35.

Gilbert, Sandra. "The American Sexual Poetics of Walt Whitman and Emily Dickinson." *Reconstructing American Literary History.* Ed. Sacvan Bercovitch. Cambridge: Harvard UP, 1986. 123–54.

———. "Feminist Criticism in the University: An Interview with Sandra Gilbert." By Gerald Graff. *Criticism in the University.* Ed. Gerald Graff and Reginald Gibbons. Chicago: Northwestern UP, 1985. 111–23.

———. "Life Studies, or, Speech After Long Silence: Feminist Critics Today." *College English* 40.8 (Apr. 1979): 849–63.

Gilligan, Carol. *In a Different Voice: Psychological Theory and Women's Development.* Cambridge: Harvard UP, 1982.

Gitlin, Todd. "Hip-Deep in Post-Modernism." *New York Times Book Review* 16 Nov. 1988: 1+.

Gordon, Deborah. "Writing Culture, Writing Feminism: The Poetics and Politics of Experimental Ethnography." *Inscriptions* 3/4 (1988): 7–24.

Grahn, Judy. *The Highest Apple: Sappho and the Lesbian Poetic Tradition.* San Francisco: Spinsters, 1985.

———. *The Queen of Wands.* Trumansburg, N.Y.: Crossing, 1982.

———. *The Work of a Common Woman.* Trumansburg, N.Y.: Crossing, 1978.

Griffin, Susan. *Made from This Earth.* New York: Harper, 1982.

———. *Woman and Nature: The Roaring Inside Her.* New York: Harper, 1978.

Hairston, Maxine. "The Winds of Change: Thomas Kuhn and the Revolution in the Teaching of Writing." *College Composition and Communication* 33 (Feb. 1982): 76–88.

Hampl, Patricia. *A Romantic Education.* Boston: Houghton, 1981.

Harari, Josue V., ed. *Textual Strategies*. Ithaca: Cornell UP, 1979.

Hartman, Geoffrey. *The Fate of Reading and Other Essays*. Chicago: U of Chicago P, 1975.

———. "Literary Commentary as Literature." *Critical Theory Since 1965*. Ed. Hazard Adams and Leroy Searle. Tallahassee: Florida State UP, 1986. 345–58.

Hassan, Ihab. "Parabiography: The Varieties of Critical Experience." *American Critics at Work*. Ed. Victor A. Kramer. Troy, N.Y.: Whitson, 1984. 421–42.

Hawthorne, Nathaniel. *The Scarlet Letter*. Boston, 1851.

Heath, Shirley Brice. "Becoming Literate in America: A Sociohistorical Perspective." *Issues in Literacy: A Research Perspective*. Ed. Jerome A. Niles and Rosary V. Lalik. Chicago: National Reading Conference, 1985. 1–18.

———. "Literacy and Language Change." *Languages and Linguistics: The Interdependence of Theory, Data, and Application*. Ed. Deborah Tannen and James E. Alatis. Washington, D.C.: Georgetown UP–Georgetown University Round Table on Languages and Linguistics, 1985. 282–93.

Hoffman, Nancy Jo. "Reading Women's Poetry: The Meaning of Our Lives." *College English* 34 (1972): 48–62.

Holden, Jonathan. *Style and Authenticity in Post-Modern Poetry*. Columbia: U of Missouri P, 1986.

Holland, Norman. "Transacting My 'Good-Morrow' or, Bringing Back the Vanished Critic." *American Critics at Work*. Ed. Victor A. Kramer. Troy, N.Y.: Whitson, 1984. 211–25.

———. "Transactive Teaching: Cordelia's Death." *College English* 39 (Nov. 1977): 276–85.

Hopkins, Gerard Manley. "Thou Art Indeed Just, Lord." *Norton Anthology of Poetry*. New York: Norton, 1975. 905–6.

Huber, Carole A. Rev. of *Teaching Writing: Pedagogy, Gender, and Equity*, ed. Cynthia Caywood and Gillian R. Overing. *College Composition and Communication* 28.3 (Oct. 1987): 355–57.

Humm, Maggie. "Feminist Criticism in America and England." *Women's Writing: A Challenge to Theory*. Ed. Moira Monteith. New York: St. Martin's, 1986. 90–116.

Irigaray, Luce. *Speculum of the Other Woman*. Trans. Gillian C. Gill. Ithaca: Cornell UP, 1985.

———. *This Sex Which Is Not One*. Trans. Catherine Porter and Carolyn Burke. Ithaca: Cornell UP, 1985.

Jacoby, Susan. "'What Do I Do for the Next Twenty Years?'" *New York Times Magazine* 17 June 1973: 10+

Janeway, Elizabeth. "Women and the Uses of Power." *The Future of Difference*. Ed. Hester Eisenstein. Boston: G. K. Hall, 1980. 327–44.

Jouve, Nicole Ward. *White Woman Speaks with Forked Tongue: Criticism as Autobiography*. London and New York: Routledge, 1991.

Juhasz, Suzanne. "The Critic as Feminist: Reflections on Women's Poetry, Feminism, and the Art of Criticism." *Women's Studies* 5 (1977): 113–27.

———. "The Journal as Source and Model for Feminist Art: The Example of Kathleen Fraser." *Frontiers* 8.1 (1984): 16–20.

Juncker, Clara. "Writing (with) Cixous." *College English* 50.4 (Apr. 1988): 424–36.

Kaplan, Caren. "Deterritorializations: The Rewriting of Home and Exile in Western Feminist Discourse." *Cultural Critique* 6 (Spring 1987): 187–98.

Kazantis, Judith. "The Errant Unicorn." *On Gender and Writing*. Ed. Michelene Wandor. London: Pandora, 1983. 24–30.

Kennard, Jean. "Personally Speaking: Feminist Critics and the Community of Readers." *College English* 43.2 (Feb. 1981): 140–45.

Kingston, Maxine Hong. *China Men*. New York: Ballatine, 1980.

———. *The Woman Warrior*. New York: Knopf, 1976.

Kramer, Victor A., ed. *American Critics at Work: Examinations of Contemporary Literary Theories*. Troy, N.Y.: Whitson, 1984.

Krieger, Murray. "Literature vs. *Écriture:* Constructions and Deconstructions in Recent Literary Theory." *American Critics at Work*. Ed. Victor A. Kramer. Troy, N.Y.: Whitson, 1984.

Kuhn, Thomas. *The Structure of Scientific Revolutions*. Vol. 2, no. 2 of *International Encyclopedia of the Unified Science*. 2d ed. Chicago: U of Chicago P, 1970.

Kumin, Maxine. *In Deep: Country Essays*. Boston: Beacon, 1988.

———. *To Make a Prairie: Essays on Poets, Poetry, and Country Living*. Ann Arbor: U of Michigan P, 1979.

Lacan, Jacques. *Ecrits: A Selection*. New York: Norton, 1977.

Leitch, Vincent. "The Book of Deconstructive Criticism." *American Critics at Work*. Ed. Victor A. Kramer. Troy, N.Y.: Whitson, 1984. 111–42.

Lesser, Wendy. "Autobiography and the 'I' of the Beholder." *New York Times Book Review* 27 Nov. 1988: 1+.

"Literal." *Webster's Third New International Dictionary.* 1976 ed.

Lorde, Audre. *The Cancer Journals.* San Francisco: Spinsters, 1980.

———. "The Evening News." *Chosen Poems—Old and New.* New York: Norton, 1982. 101.

———. *Sister Outsider: Essays and Speeches.* Trumansburg, N.Y.: Crossing, 1984.

Lugones, Maria C., and Elizabeth V. Spelman. "Have We Got a Theory for You! Feminist Theory, Cultural Imperialism and the Demand for 'The Women's Voice.'" *Women's Studies International Forum* 6.6 (1983): 573–81.

Mairs, Nancy. "On Being a Cripple." *Plaintext: Deciphering a Woman's Life.* New York: Harper, 1986. 9–20.

———. *Remembering the Bone House: An Erotics of Place and Space.* New York: Harper, 1989.

Mander, Anica. *Feminism as Therapy.* New York: Random, 1974.

Marks, Elaine, and Isabelle de Courtivron. *New French Feminisms.* Amherst: U of Massachusetts P, 1980.

Marvell, Andrew. "A Dialogue Between the Soul and the Body." *The Norton Anthology of Poetry.* Ed. Alexander Allison et al. New York: Norton, 1975. 366.

Miller, Nancy K. *Getting Personal: Feminist Occasions and Other Autobiographical Acts.* London and New York: Routledge, 1991.

Mitchell, Juliet, and Jacqueline Rose, eds. *Feminine Sexuality: Jacques Lacan and the Ecole Freudienne.* New York: Norton, 1982.

Moi, Toril. *Sexual/Textual Politics: Feminist Literary Theory.* London: Methuen, 1985.

Monteith, Moira. Introduction. *Women's Writing: A Challenge to Theory.* Ed. Moira Monteith. New York: St. Martin's, 1986. 1–9.

Moraga, Cherrie. *Loving in the War Years.* Boston: South End, 1983.

Moran, Charles. "Teaching Writing/Teaching Literature." *College Composition and Communication* 46 (Dec. 1984): 756–66.

Myerson, Joel. "Sarah Margaret Fuller." *The Heath Anthology of American Literature.* Ed. Paul Lauter et al. Lexington, Mass.: D.C. Heath, 1990. 1580–83.

Oakley, Anne. *Taking It Like a Woman.* New York: Random, 1984.

Olsen, Tillie. *Silences*. New York: Dell, 1978.

Penelope (Stanley), Julia, and Susan J. Wolfe. "Consciousness as Style; Style as Aesthetic." *Language, Gender, and Society: A Second Decade of Research*. Ed. Barrie Thorne, Cheris Kramarae, and Nancy Henley. Rowley, Mass.: Newbury, 1983. 125–39.

Peterson, Bruce. "Writing about Responses: A Unified Model of Reading, Interpretation, and Composition." *College English* 44.5 (Sept. 1982): 459–68.

Petrosky, Anthony R. "From Story to Essay: Reading and Writing." *College Composition and Communication* 33 (1982): 19–35.

Piercy, Marge. *Circles on the Water*. New York: Knopf, 1982.

———. "Out of the Rubbish." *My Mother's Body: Poems*. New York: Knopf, 1985. 11.

———. *Parti-Colored Blocks for a Quilt*. Ann Arbor: U of Michigan P, 1986.

———. *The Twelve-Spoked Wheel Flashing*. New York: Knopf, 1978.

Pinsky, Robert. "Poet Robert Pinsky: Seeking Roots of Courage in the Human Heart." Interview. *Boston University Alumni Today* Apr.–June 1989: 8.

Plath, Sylvia. *The Collected Poems*. New York: Harper, 1981.

Rabben, Linda. "Other Selves, Other Lives." Rev. of *Brazilian Women Speak: Contemporary Life Stories*, by Daphne Patai. *Women's Review of Books* 6.4 (Jan. 1989): 15–16.

Rich, Adrienne. *Blood, Bread, and Poetry: Selected Prose 1979–1985*. New York: Norton, 1986.

———. *The Fact of a Doorframe: Poems Selected and New 1950–1984*. New York: Norton, 1984.

———. *Of Woman Born: Motherhood as Experience and Institution*. New York: Norton, 1976.

———. *On Lies, Secrets, and Silence: Selected Prose 1966–1978*. New York: Norton, 1978.

———. *Sources*. Woodside, Calif.: Heyeck, 1983.

Roethke, Theodore. "Elegy for Jane." *The Collected Poems*. Garden City, N.Y.: Anchor-Doubleday, 1975. 98.

Rose, Phyllis. *Writing of Women: Essays in a Renaissance*. Rev. ed. Middletown, Conn.: Wesleyan UP, 1986.

Rosenblatt, Louise. *Literature as Exploration*. New York: Appleton-Century, 1938. New York: MLA, 1976.

Ruddick, Sara. "Maternally Thinking." *Feminist Studies* 6 (Summer 1980): 342–67.

Russ, Joanna. *How to Suppress Women's Writing*. Austin: U of Texas P, 1983.

Ruth, Sheila. "A Serious Look at Consciousness-Raising." *Social Theory and Practice* 2 (Spring 1973): 289–300.

Ryan, Barbara. "Chrysalis: A Thesis Journal." Diss. U of Washington, 1988.

Salvatori, Mariolina. "Reading and Writing a Text: Correlations Between Reading and Writing Patterns." *College English* 45.7 (Nov. 1983): 657–66.

Scholes, Robert. *Textual Power.* New Haven: Yale UP, 1985.

Schweickart, Patrocinio. "Reading Ourselves: Toward a Feminist Theory of Reading." *Gender and Reading: Essays on Readers, Texts, and Contexts.* Ed. Elizabeth A. Flynn and Patrocinio Schweickart. Baltimore: Johns Hopkins UP, 1986. 31–62.

Sexton, Anne. *The Complete Poems.* Boston: Houghton, 1981.

Showalter, Elaine. "Feminist Criticism in the Wilderness." *The New Feminist Criticism: Essays on Women, Literature, and Theory.* Ed. Elaine Showalter. New York: Pantheon, 1985. 243–70.

"Sonnet." *Oxford English Dictionary.* 1971 ed.

Steinfels, Peter. "Battle Lines on Feminist and Religion." *New York Times* 10 May 1989: A14.

Stimpson, Catherine. *Where the Meanings Are: Feminism and Cultural Spaces.* New York: Methuen, 1988.

Stull, William. "Literature, Literary Theory, and the Teaching of Composition." *Research in Composition and Rhetoric: A Bibliographic Sourcebook.* Ed. Michael G. Moran and Ronald F. Lunsford. Westport, Conn.: Greenwood, 1984. 125–52.

Sukenick, Lynn. "On Women and Fiction." *The Authority of Experience.* Ed. Lee Edwards and Arlyn Diamond. Amherst: U of Massachusetts P, 1977. 33–44.

Thorne, Barrie, Cheris Kramarae, and Nancy Henley, eds. *Language, Gender, and Society: A Second Decade of Research.* Rowley, Mass.: Newbury, 1983.

Todd, Janet. *Feminist Literary History.* New York: Routledge, 1988.

Tompkins, Jane. "Criticism and Feeling." *College English* 39.2 (Oct. 1977): 169–78.

———. "Me and My Shadow." *New Literary History* 19.1 (Fall 1987): 169–85.

Torsney, Cheryl B. "Me and My Essay: A Proposal for a New Academic Essay Written in My Own Voice." *The Intimate Critique: Autobiographical Literary Criticism.* Ed. Diane Freedman, Olivia Frey, and Frances Zauhar. Durham: Duke UP, forthcoming.

Vendler, Helen. *The Music of What Happens*. Cambridge: Harvard UP, 1988.

Von Hallberg, Robert. "American Poet-Critics Since 1945." *Reconstructing American Literary History*. Ed. Sacvan Bercovitch. Cambridge: Harvard UP, 1986. 280–99.

Wakoski, Diane. "Bodily Fluent." Rev. of *Available Light,* by Marge Piercy. *Women's Review of Books* 5.10–11 (July 1988): 7–8.

Walker, Alice. "Everyday Use." *In Love and Trouble: Stories of Black Women*. New York: Harcourt, 1967. 47–59.

———. *In Search of Our Mothers' Gardens*. New York: Harcourt, 1983.

———. *Revolutionary Petunias*. New York: Harcourt, 1973.

Wandor, Michelene. "Voices are Wild." *Women's Writing: A Challenge to Theory*. Ed. Moira Monteith. New York: St. Martin's, 1986. 72–89.

Whitman, Walt. "Song of Myself." *Leaves of Grass*. Ed. Harold W. Blodgett and Sculley Bradley. New York: Norton, 1965. 28–89.

Yeats, William Butler. "A Dialogue of Self and Soul." *The Norton Anthology of Modern Poetry*. Ed. Richard Ellmann and Robert O'Clair. New York: Norton, 1973. 144.

Index